Keeping Graduate Programs Responsive to National Needs

Michael J. Pelczar, Jr., Lewis C. Solmon, *Editors*

Published in collaboration with the Institute of Industrial Relations, University of California, Los Angeles and the Council of Graduate Schools of the United States.

NEW DIRECTIONS FOR HIGHER EDUCATION

MARTIN KRAMER, *Editor-in-Chief*

Number 46, June 1984

Paperback sourcebooks in
The Jossey-Bass Higher Education Series

D1092015

Jossey-Bass Inc., Publishers
San Francisco • Washington • London

Michael J. Pelczar, Jr., Lewis C. Solmon (Eds.).
Keeping Graduate Programs Responsive to National Needs.
New Directions for Higher Education, no. 46.
Volume XII, number 3.
San Francisco: Jossey-Bass, 1984.

New Directions for Higher Education Series
Martin Kramer, *Editor-in-Chief*

New Directions for Higher Education (publication number USPS
990-880) is published quarterly by Jossey-Bass Inc., Publishers.
New Directions is numbered sequentially—please order extra
copies by sequential number. The volume and issue numbers
above are included for the convenience of libraries. Second-class
postage rates paid at San Francisco, California, and at
additional mailing offices.

Correspondence:
Subscriptions, single-issue orders, change of address notices, undelivered
copies, and other correspondence should be sent to Subscriptions,
Jossey-Bass Inc., Publishers, 433 California Street, San Francisco,
California 94104.

Editorial correspondence should be sent to the Consulting Editor,
Martin Kramer, 2807 Shasta Road, Berkeley, California 94708.

Library of Congress Catalogue Card Number LC 83-82811
International Standard Serial Number ISSN 0271-0560
International Standard Book Number ISBN 87589-996-X

Cover art by Willi Baum
Manufactured in the United States of America

Ordering Information

The paperback sourcebooks listed below are published quarterly and can be ordered either by subscription or as single copies.

Subscriptions cost $35.00 per year for institutions, agencies, and libraries. Individuals can subscribe at the special rate of $25.00 per year *if payment is by personal check.* (Note that the full rate of $35.00 applies if payment is by institutional check, even if the subscription is designated for an individual.) Standing orders are accepted.

Single copies are available at $8.95 when payment accompanies order, and *all single-copy orders under $25.00 must include payment.* (California, Washington, D.C., New Jersey, and New York residents please include appropriate sales tax.) For billed orders, cost per copy is $8.95 plus postage and handling. (Prices subject to change without notice.)

Bulk orders (ten or more copies) of any individual sourcebook are available at the following discounted prices: 10–49 copies, $8.05 each; 50–100 copies, $7.15 each; over 100 copies, *inquire.* Sales tax and postage and handling charges apply as for single copy orders.

To ensure correct and prompt delivery, all orders must give either the *name of an individual* or an *official purchase order number.* Please submit your order as follows:

Subscriptions: specify series and subscription year.
Single Copies: specify sourcebook code and issue number (such as, HE8).

Mail orders for United States and Possessions, Latin America, Canada, Japan, Australia, and New Zealand to:
Jossey-Bass Inc., Publishers
433 California Street
San Francisco, California 94104

Mail orders for all other parts of the world to:
Jossey-Bass Limited
28 Banner Street
London EC1Y 8QE

New Directions for Higher Education Series
Martin Kramer, *Editor-in-Chief*

Contents

Introduction

This volume is a timely addition to the literature on graduate education. We have heard there are "signs of trouble and erosion in graduate education," and that, unless our graduate schools receive the support they require, they will not be able to respond to the nation's imperatives and expectations.

In the chapters presented here, we find helpful information concerning the state of graduate education, the assessment of quality in innovative graduate programs, and the significance of certain new trends such as industry-university partnerships in research and development. There are also interesting ideas about new career opportunities for recipients of graduate degrees.

Several of the chapters in this sourcebook point out that the assessment of quality, particularly in innovative graduate programs, is too often based only on the traditional grounds of institutional or departmental reputation. The achievement of substance in such evaluations is, of course, more complicated than that. As David S. Webster notes in one of his rubrics, there is "evidence that innovation is punished." It is certainly true, for example, that attempts to offer new professional programs at the master's level sometimes encounter severe handicaps when confronted by the traditional practices of some professional accrediting bodies. Such practices make it important that there be a clearer understanding about the relationship between innovative programs and traditional perspectives of quality in graduate education.

Bryce Jordan
President
Pennsylvania State University

Editors' Notes

This volume is the result of the merging of two interests: the desire of the Council of Graduate Schools in the United States to document the development of new graduate programs in institutions across the country, and the UCLA Institute of Industrial Relations's interest in how universities are adapting their offerings to new needs of the labor market. Although it is apparent that some of what is put forth as innovation is merely repackaging and relabeling of what has been going on for many years, it is clear that a great deal of substantive change is also occurring in graduate education. This volume considers both the process and the result of recent innovation.

The volume begins with a look, by Pelczar and Frances, at how graduate education has evolved to the present, an assessment of changing conditions, and suggestions for new directions for the future. Chapters by Albrecht and Solmon look at the process of innovation, how it might occur, and what the potential barriers to change are. In the next two chapters, Webster and Millard discuss issues in the assessment of the quality of innovative graduate programs.

Following these general statements, the chapters by Fulton, Schneider, and Dieter specifically consider innovations in the fields of humanities, education, and engineering, respectively. In Chapter Nine, Passer provides an example of technological innovation for curricular enhancement, and then Kersey looks at new career opportunities in the business world for those traditionally educated for academic positions. Next, LaPidus discusses the capabilities of graduate education to provide international perspectives. Chapters by Young and Khoury then look at different aspects of graduate education vis-a-vis the nontraditional student.

A major new thrust in graduate programs has been to build links with industry. This industry-university partnership is discussed in the chapter by Seferis and Williams. Finally, Linney evaluates the role of the federal government in graduate program innovation. Bowen concludes the volume with his views of the social responsibility of graduate education.

The editors thank Nancy Tookey of UCLA, who served as research assistant for this series of essays, and acknowledge the support of the Council of Graduate Schools in the United States, the UCLA Institute of Industrial Relations, and the UCLA Graduate School of Education.

1

It seems clear that we still do not have a definitive answer on whether graduate eduation has been sufficiently responsive to changing labor market requirements and to other societal needs. The contributors to this volume have provided insight into what has occurred to date. We invite interested readers to correspond with the editors about additional innovations we have not included. This volume is a beginning effort to document attempts at change. More of the success stories must be disseminated as role models for others. The problems that are being faced must be made known so that barriers can be surmounted.

During a period when support for graduate education is predicated on how well its institutions are serving the nation, it is vital that eduational leaders provide ways to meet the changing requirements of all the recipients of educational benefits. We hope that this publication takes some steps toward this purpose.

Michael J. Pelczar, Jr.
Lewis C. Solmon
Editors

Michael J. Pelczar, Jr., is president of the Council of Graduate Schools in the United States.

Lewis C. Solmon is associate dean and professor in the Graduate School of Education, University of California, Los Angeles.

*Graduate education faces the task of adapting to changes in
the greater society, so that its traditional influence may not
only be maintained but broadened.*

Graduate Education: Past
Performance and Future Direction

Michael J. Pelczar, Jr.
Carol Frances

Graduate degrees have been awarded for the past 800 years. The
University of Bologna (Italy) is credited with conferring the first doctoral degree in the middle of the twelfth century. Yale University
granted the first Ph.D. in the United States in 1861. Johns Hopkins
University followed in 1876 with the establishment of the first traditional graduate education program. Since that event, a period of
approximately 100 years, graduate education has become the center-
piece of our nation's system of education. It has emerged to play a
special role in supporting our economy, our culture, our security, our
professions—in short, our way of life. Internationally, the graduate
school in the United States is viewed by many as the graduate school of
the world.

In the last ten years we have witnessed a significant slowing
down and, in some areas, an actual decline of graduate education
activities. Total enrollments have remained essentially constant, but
graduate student support has been sharply cut back; federally supported fellowships dropped from 80,000 in 1969 to less than 20,000 in
1982. This overall downturn has led, in part, to the establishment of a

M. J. Pelczar, L. C. Solmon (Eds.). *Keeping Graduate Programs Responsive to National Needs.*
New Directions for Higher Education, no. 46. San Francisco: Jossey-Bass, June 1984.

graduate education subcommittee of the National Commission on Student Financial Assistance (1983). The title of the commission's report reflects the present condition: *Signs of Trouble and Erosion: A Report on Graduate Education in America.*

The Comprehensive Nature of Graduate Education

Graduate education, as developed in the United States, is very comprehensive, embracing all advanced degree work beyond the baccalaureate. Useful distinctions are sometimes made between first professional degrees and graduate degrees in the arts and sciences; however, in many subject areas, the distinction between an academically oriented program and a professional or practitioner-type program is becoming increasingly blurred.

Four hundred fifty-two institutions offer both the earned doctorate and the master's degree. Approximately 423 institutions offer the master's degree as their highest degree, and another 139 offer degrees beyond the master's but less than the doctorate. Private and public institutions share the graduate education load, with private institutions enrolling 59 percent of the professional students and the public institutions enrolling 68 percent of the students in the other components of graduate education.

Highlights of Graduate Education's Evolution

The Master's Degree. Graduate education at the master's level has undergone many changes since the first Master of Arts degree was awarded by the University of Paris in the twelfth century. The degree's meaning and value over the years have fluctuated. Originally, the Master of Arts degree designated a licensed teacher in the faculty of the arts. A period of time followed when the master's degree was awarded more or less automatically to anyone who was in good academic standing one to three years after receiving a baccalaureate degree. During the nineteenth century efforts were made to restore this degree to an earned status; in the mid 1800s, for example, the University of Michigan became the first major American university to restore the status of the master's degree. In the 1930s, the degree achieved a new level of significance as colleges and universities expanded their programs in education to prepare larger numbers of teachers; in 1939 it was estimated that three-fourths of liberal arts master's degrees were earned by public school teachers. This trend continued for the next two decades.

A more recent trend has been the growth of practitioner or career-oriented programs at the master's level. Such degrees include: Master of Social Work (M.S.W.), Master of Theater Arts (M.T.A.), Master of Law and Taxation (M.L.T.), Master of Library Science (M.L.S.), and Master of Industrial Design (M.I.D.). Several hundred different titles of master's degrees are now in use.

The largest number of master's degrees awarded was 317,164 in 1976-77. This compares with 208,291 in 1969-70 and 74,497 in 1959-60. There has been a slight but gradual decrease since 1977; the number awarded in 1981-82 was 295,546. The distribution is approximately even between men and women. The number of master's degrees awarded to minority students was 30,418 in 1976-76 and 30,910 in 1980-81.

A major issue associated with master's programs is that of assessing their quality. The extremely large number of programs and their great diversity in subject content and differences in objectives complicate the process of program evaluation. This is an issue that needs more attention by the graduate community, particularly since programs with an applied, career-oriented focus are on the increase. The Council of Graduate Schools in the United States (1975) states:

> Broadly speaking, the master's degree indicates that the holder has mastered a program in a particular field sufficiently to pursue creative projects in that specialty. In some areas, it may be a prerequisite for further study toward a more advanced degree such as the doctorate. The degree should be awarded for completion of a coherent program designed to assure the mastery of specified knowledge and skills, rather than for the random accumulation of a certain number of course credits after attaining the baccalaureate [p. 1-2].

The Doctoral Degree. By 1960, the number of doctorates awarded reached the 10,000 mark. However, it was the next ten-year period that produced an explosion at this level of graduate education. In 1970-71, 32,107 doctoral degrees were awarded, 27,530 to men and 4,577 to women. The peak year was 1974-75 with 34,086 degrees awarded, 26,819 to men and 7,267 to women. Since then, the number of doctorates awarded has shown a slight but steady decrease. However, there has been a sharp increase in the number of women recipients; in 1981-82, 10,483 women earned doctorates out of a total of 32,707. The number of minority doctorate recipients was 2,285 in 1975-76 and 2,751 in 1980-81.

The National Research Council in its report of earned doctorates (1983) lists forty-six research and applied research degree titles in addition to the Ph.D. (Professional degrees such as the M.D., D.D.S., O.D., D.V.M., and J.D. are not included.) The total number of doctorates awarded annually has changed very little since 1971, but the relative constancy of this figure obscures significant decreases in selected areas. Between 1971 and 1981, for example, the number of new doctorates awarded decreased in the major categories of engineering (down 30 percent), mathematics (down 39 percent), physical sciences (down 32 percent), and foreign languages (down 18 percent).

The Present Environment

The graduate education subcommittee of the National Commission on Student Financial Assistance (1983) reports that "unless our graduate schools receive the support they require, they will not be able to respond to the nation's imperatives and expectations" (p. 11).

Universities today, like many other sectors of our society, are confronted with a multitude of problems. These problems are of two general kinds — namely, resources (the need for adequate long-term support) and attitude and social responsibility (the acceptance by the university community of the necessity of adapting to changes in the greater society so that its traditional influence may be not only maintained but possibly broadened).

Resources. Universities are falling behind in replacing essential research and instructional equipment; library collections and services have not kept pace with student needs; faculty salaries have fallen substantially below inflation rates. Universities have felt the impact of reduced federal support, with federal revenues dropping appreciably between 1970 and 1980. During this decade, public universities experienced a reduction from 24 to 16 percent of their total revenues from federal funds, and federal funding at private universities dropped from 33 to 27 percent.

Some states have done reasonably well in assisting selected graduate-level professional schools, but their support for graduate work in other areas has been merged with undergraduate funding. The states' policies are not likely to change at this time, since states have had to adjust their budgets to accommodate federal aid cuts during a time of widespread recession. A recent survey reveals that half of the fifty states expect their spending to exceed their incomes in 1983.

Attitude and Social Responsibility. It will take more than additional financial and physical resources to address the broad issues confronting graduate education today. There is also a need for a new commitment by the university community to social responsibility. As

Howard Bowen states in the last chapter in this sourcebook, the social responsibility of a department or school is twofold: (1) an obligation to graduate competent practitioners and (2) an "obligation to turn out men and women of broad learning and culture who will join the leadership of the society and will exert constructive influences in community and civic life."

The transition from an industrial society to an information society; changes in demography; the rapidity of technological advances; new partnerships among business, industry, and academia; and greater internationalization of our activities; these and other changes call for modifications in our educational practices, procedures, and programs. For example, by the end of the 1980s, the age group consisting of eighteen- to twenty-four-year-olds will decrease by four million, and the age group twenty-five and over will increase by 22.9 million. This "adult" group has a real need for postbaccalaureate education and training. How will it be provided? There is an urgent need for more cooperative efforts, not only within the university but also with constituencies outside the university. How are these to be accommodated? There is a growing need for education and training of students across disciplines; new curriculum arrangements are needed. These and other conditions call for a new order of academic leadership — leadership that might best be formulated by new joint efforts of administration and faculty.

William D. McElroy (1978), former chancellor of the University of California, San Diego and former director of the National Science Foundation, has stressed the need for anticipating change in graduate education:

> Our society — and indeed the world — requires more, not less, of the highest-quality people from our graduate schools. To meet this requirement, we will have to change our patterns somewhat, institute some new programs, and take some modest risks. . . . Despite the inertia of our academically conservative faculty and the glacier-like movement of our academic institutions, we will probably make many corrections in course, and a decade from now, one will note considerable differences on the American graduate education scene.

In remarks entitled "The Post-Gutenburg University," Dr. Steven Muller (1983), president of Johns Hopkins University, told the American Association for Higher Education that "we are already in an environment for higher education that represents the most drastic change since the founding of the great European universities some eight or nine centuries ago. In the decades to come, the university will be serving a new clientele, delivering services in new ways, and re-examining what and how it teaches. Within five years," he warned, "the faculty may not understand how their students are learning. The most serious problem may be a post-Gutenberg university with a pre-Gutenberg faculty."

Most recently, David Saxon (1983), chairman of the board of Massachusetts Institute of Technology and former president of the University of California, told the annual meeting of the National Association of State Universities and Land-Grant Colleges:

> The pace today is so rapid in so many fields that the requirements for providing students with a truly fundamental base of knowledge on which they can build for the future constantly change. The pressure, in short, is inexorably for flexibility of academic programs and, even more importantly, for flexibility of people — not least in the faculties and staffs of our own institutions....
>
> In the years ahead we will have larger numbers of non-traditional students taught in a greater variety of nontraditional ways.... Finding the right mechanism for meaningful new educational arrangements will require time and experimentation, but it is imperative that the process begin.

Impact of Research Trends on Graduate Education

Historically, teaching and research have been more closely linked in the United States than in any other country. The generation of new knowledge has been intertwined with the transmission of existing knowledge as faculty combine teaching and research, and most graduate students participate in research projects while they complete their degree requirements.

These interconnections have contributed to the great scientific and technological strength of this country. Now, and in the future, the funding of research is of critical importance to the vitality of graduate education.

In the past, colleges and universities have performed close to half of the basic research in this country. They accounted for $2 billion of the $4 billion spent on basic research in the United States in 1977. Over the five years that followed, basic research grew by $507 million. Of this increase, however, the colleges and universities accounted for only 37 percent. This share of the added dollars of research showed a significant drop from the 50 percent share of total research monies used by colleges and universities in 1977.

The direction and momentum of these changes in the patterns of research performance and funding indicate that higher education is in the process of losing a part of its share of the basic research market to industry.

This trend could have significant implications for the future of graduate education. Industry is increasing the resources it has to perform basic research as a result of its own increased spending on research and of increased federal research dollars channeled to industry. As a result, industry will have greater drawing power in attracting top researchers from academic institutions into industrial research laboratories. Narrowing the gap between the older research equipment in the educational institutions and the new equipment in the industrial research laboratories will become increasingly difficult. This could portend a cycle of still further erosion of the college and university share of basic research — to the future detriment of graduate education.

The Future

Because graduate education serves a national purpose, a strongly sustained national commitment toward graduate education is needed. Agriculture is one area in which federal support for research and education has been consistent, dating back to legislation that complemented the Morrill Act (land-grant colleges) of 1862. Every state has chartered, approved, or established one or more universities — but rarely with a clear conception of graduate education in mind. Collectively, the states' educational policies do not constitute a national perspective or policy on graduate education.

Graduate education is the nation's principal wellspring of new knowledge and techniques in the basic disciplines and in the professions. This new knowledge has been essential to the growth of our economy, to our defense and security, and to our personal and social well-being. Universities have played a principal role in interpreting and communicating new knowledge to individuals, to the representatives of local, state, and national governments and their agencies, to the business and industrial community, and to the professions. No other nation depends upon its universities as extensively as we do.

The luxury of procrastination and short-term planning for graduate education has run its course. The development of an institution to university status requires many years of time and much effort. Continued delay in reaching a strong national commitment to graduate education will reduce the preeminence of this nation in nearly all basic disciplines and in the professions. We face the challenge of establishing a framework of financial and popular support that will maintain graduate education at a level that excels that of any other nation. Unless this commitment is realized, our national aspirations relating to political stability, economic viability, national security, and humane values will be in jeopardy.

References

Council of Graduate Schools in the United States. *The Master's Degree.* Washington, D.C.: Council of Graduate Schools in the United States, 1975.

Council of Graduate Schools in the United States. *Proceedings of the Annual Meetings* (Vol 18). Washington, D.C.: Council of Graduate Schools in the United States, 1978.

Muller, S. "The Post-Gutenberg University." Paper presented to the American Association for Higher Education, Spring 1983.

National Commission on Student Financial Assistance. *Signs of Trouble and Erosion: A Report on Graduate Education in America.* New York: New York University, 1983.

National Research Council, Office of Scientific and Engineering Personnel. *Summary Report, 1982—Doctorate Recipients from United States Universities.* Washington, D.C.: National Academy Press, 1983.

Michael J. Pelczar, Jr., is president of the Council of Graduate Schools in the United States.

Carol Frances is chief economic adviser to the National Education Industry Group of Coopers and Lybrand.

The organization and procedures of universities make it
tempting to try to avoid contemporary challenges to
graduate education.

Opportunity and Impediment in Graduate Program Innovation

Paul A. Albrecht

Demand and opportunity for innovation in graduate education abound, coming both from inside and outside universities. Stabilizing or declining enrollments; dramatically shifting enrollment patterns; rapid developments in technology; shifting clientele to older, returning, midcareer students; and changing, often declining, financial support from a variety of causes, coupled with the national need to revitalize the economy—all lead to a need for substantial change. Problems are gaining; opportunities beckon. But these factors merely suggest change; they by no means guarantee it. For effective innovation to occur, educational institutions must be capable of change. An examination of the propensity for innovation is in order.

These are perhaps both the worst of times and best of times for graduate program innovation. They are the worst of times because shrinking resources and stable or declining enrollments generate an almost overwhelming emphasis on solidifying programs, or even on retrenching and eliminating programs, in order to contain the erosion of quality and to meet prior commitments (notably those to tenured faculty). They are the best of times because need and threat are typically essential ingredients of the will to change. Also, current opportuni-

M. J. Pelczar, L. C. Solmon (Eds.). *Keeping Graduate Programs Responsive to National Needs.*
New Directions for Higher Education, no. 46. San Francisco: Jossey-Bass, June 1984.

ties can potentially engage powerful individual and common commitment because these opportunities represent national needs — for economic development, international competitiveness, and societal adaptation. Too seldom is it recognized that failure to change also has significant costs — costs that typically only become evident later. In the international marketplace, for example, American firms are becoming painfully aware of such opportunity costs.

Universities, as now conceived, organized, and directed, are not particularly well suited to innovation and change in educational performance. This problem is perceived to a degree by the general public, which increasingly regards higher education as defensive, self-serving, inappropriately arrogant with lay persons, and behind the times. In the area of research, universities show a much higher rate of innovation, and research is therefore the glory of the university. But in the area of education, as distinguished from research, the rate of real and effective innovation in established universities is in fact very low.

Alternatives to Innovation — The First Impediments of Change

The "Retreat." When confronting the possibility of making significant adaptations, rather than merely tinkering at the margin, faculty and administrators in universities are tempted by one available retreat and one detour. The retreat is to propose (and to feel) that the traditional approach is, after all, the best way to meet new educational and career needs, if only the clients and the public were enlightened enough to realize this. The implication is that one of the main functions of graduate education is to develop at a high level disciplined, analytical, and creative thinking and the skills of systematic investigation. These certainly, it is stated, are core attributes of effective performance in a wide variety of functions and careers. Nothing in the end is as practical as a good theory. Thus, the argument sets up education as the opposite of mere training, emphasizing fundamentals in contrast to things mechanistic and what is enduring as opposed to what is trendy.

There is, of course, substance as well as retreat in this argument. When intelligent, talented, and capable people successfully complete the rigors of a research doctorate program, there are indeed alternative careers of varying sorts in which they can make a significant contribution and in which they can succeed. Recent attempts to broaden the range of options known to and considered by Ph.D. recipients are highly desirable. Furthermore, fundamental analytical sophistication does indeed provide the basis for competence in many functions.

But this approach to meeting new educational, research, and career needs is too simple, cumbersome, and unfocused, and it has the effect of increasing the resistance to change. Linkages between fundamentals and different subject areas, careers, and clients are absolutely essential, but creating these linkages in an effective manner may require substantial adaptation. Inevitably (although often to the surprise of persons in the university), clients and the public do not rally in support of the mere extension of familiar approaches into new territory. In fact, when continuance of the conventions is all that is proposed to meet new needs, mutual alienation and misunderstanding frequently develop.

The "Detour." This attitude looks at innovation almost exclusively within the framework of quality. Since there is a major concern about quality in education, a distinct possibility exists that innovation will in fact be swamped by a preoccupation with quality. In theory, quality and innovation are inextricably intertwined and mutually supportive, but, in practice, the strategy of innovation becomes more complex and may be obsured and inhibited by quality considerations.

When those responsible for graduate education think of quality, they tend, amost instinctively, to approach the matter in terms of the quality with which current programs guided by current educational concepts are implemented. The new or different, then, is automatically suspect. For example, state commissions now give a very searching evaluation of proposed new programs, almost reflexly regarding them as unwarranted proliferation. In a time of retrenchment, this attitude is accentuated. In fact, one of the unfortunate effects of the need to retrench is the tendency to fine-tune the past. In a volatile time, this one-sided approach can be unproductive, even dangerous, because it may lead to a failure to capitalize on needed redirection and change. That is, while cutting literal current costs, heavy opportunity costs may be accepted.

A factor that leads to confusion when quality and innovation are considered simultaneously is a tendency to take a truncated view of quality. Quality certainly should involve doing the right or appropriate things well, not merely doing better what always has been done. That is, it involves both ends and means. The conventional view is to take the ends for granted and to concentrate on the means.

In this regard, four loci of quality in graduate education merit consideration: (1) the ability and preparation of students at entrance; (2) the stature and appropriateness of the faculty; (3) the program design, including the curricular objectives; and (4) the effectiveness in fact of the implementation of program design. In other words, quality is a function of students, faculty, program concept, and effectiveness in application. We frequently measure the first two, occasionally the last, and rarely the third. Innovation, conversely, involves a significant attention to program concept; to a degree, it changes the emphasis in looking at quality from faculty to program concept and effectiveness in application. This shift in emphasis often is not made.

Merely to continue to do what we have always done, even to do better what we have always done, is in many areas to shrink and to become increasingly out of date. Those emphasizing the quality strategy for survival speak to issues such as the importance of value added and received, the respect of society for a service, and competitive survival in a traditional pool in a difficult time. But they do speak well, typically, to meeting new needs and to the enlargement of vision and function.

Longstanding Disincentives to Innovation

The opportunities that impinge upon us and that should entice, invigorate, and stimulate us have fundamentally two dimensions: (1) those stemming from the continuing explosion of knowledge that creates new educational needs and careers and (2) those arising from new populations seeking and needing graduate education. Inevitably, these dimensions are frequently insufficient to provide quality education in light of these changes.

If we are to concentrate on innovation through program design and strategy, we have formidable obstacles to overcome. Institutions have shrunk from innovation not merely from lack of thought or interest; there are also significant barriers and disincentives. Some of them are in fact long-held and valued explicit strategies, some are largely implicit attitudes, and some are fundamental structural and resource limitations. Some may even be impossible to change in the short run. But it may be instructive to look at a few of them briefly. Some rearrangement, even if only at the margin, is usually possible.

Strategies That Inhibit Change. Two key strategies come to mind as barriers to innovation. They are not wrong, merely partially right. Most strategic assessment and planning, in fact, involves the analysis of trade-offs, of partial truths.

The first is the strategy of building strength on strength. Concentration is the byword. Do a few things well. In a time of retrenchment, this strategy gains renewed support. Who can argue against such wise strategy, frequently a favorite of governing boards and state commissions? Certainly most observers agree that graduate education suffers from overproliferation of programs and should concentrate its strengths. But there is a problem with this approach, particularly if one means by "strength," faculty strength. For institutional effectiveness of a high order, it requires a parallel strategy of courageous elimination of programs—a strategy rarely followed courageously or otherwise. If there is no such combination, the institution concentrates on doing well or better things that it is already doing. New things, or even the major redesign of old things, are precluded in the interest of strengthening the past.

A second strategy, widely held in quality institutions, is that a new or different area should only be entered in force with high, mature quality evident almost immediately—as if William Rainey Harper's hookup with John D. Rockefeller's resources in the early days of the University of Chicago were modal. One school examined the formation of a law school, for example, for reasons that are obscure. In so doing, some distinguished faculty members suggested very strongly that, unless the proposed law school could compete immediately with the three or four top schools in the country, the university should not attempt to start the new school. Of course, it did not try; to set up the school in this way would have been prohibitively expensive.

But, pushed to an extreme, this partial truth is nonsense and would result in very little ever being built except in the most extremely favorable of circumstances. Even the top three or four schools were not built that way themselves initially. While it is wise to count the cost before starting on a new or largely redesigned venture, almost all emergent activities and institutions are somewhat shaky at the start and follow the learning curve. This process needs to be accepted.

Attitudinal Barriers. A formidable barrier to the inclination to focus on design is a common snobbishness about clients. There is a clear preference built into graduate systems for full-time, mainline, conventional-age students. At the graduate level, the preference is for students who wish to recapitulate faculty careers. Faculty prefer to teach themselves thirty years younger. The preference also is for the students to be so bright and well prepared that faculty are hardly necessary. A related set of status commitments prefers theoretical over applied programs, vertical specialization over breadth, and established over emergent programs.

Yet many of the opportunities over the next decade lie elsewhere. Minority students, foreign students, part-time students, mid-career students, and re-entry students represent the growth areas. Elite, or even merely solid, quality institutions assign these students to institutions down the status ladder, which they regard as of lesser quality. This may in some ways be a reasonable division of labor, notably in highly complex, vertical disciplines in which the very young often make the seminal contributions. But the result of this snobbishness and status preoccupation is that even lower-ranked institutions approach these students half-heartedly and grudgingly. All institutions should be experimenting to a degree, developing model programs, and keeping their hand in these growth areas — to the benefit of society as well as of their own institutions. In certain subject areas, as in applied and professionally oriented ones, these students are in fact often superior.

Another closely related attitude is a tendency to confuse packaging with substance, delivery system with content, familar structures with goals. This attitude leads to heavy and frequently unwarranted inferences about the quality from such attributes as full- or part-time study, time of day of classes, and conventionality of ostensible educational goals. To be sure, if the program is designed for the usual mode, as in the case of full-time study, the students will appear to be — in fact, likely will be — in an inferior position if they cannot fit into these conventional structures comfortably.

But suppose the program were deliberately and carefully designed to meet a different situation? It would be expensive if done correctly, but there are examples of such carefully designed systems. Some of the adaptations may have to be rather radical. At the Claremont Graduate School, we have an entirely separate set of credit and degree programs for 300 experienced managers and executives in the public and private sectors. The program is run on a matrix basis and has no assigned full-time faculty of its own, although it does have faculty governing committees of the usual sort made up of full-time faculty elsewhere in the institution. It has an executive director as combined administrative-academic head and a rather elaborate additional administrative staff. Faculty sometimes are assigned part of their loads in the program, sometimes teach in it on an internal overload basis, and some adjunct faculty, notably in highly specialized areas, are used. In addition to the expected home disciplines of the faculty for such a program, faculty are drawn from psychology, international relations, history, philosophy, information science, and the like.

Faculty who do not work out are not asked back. Every course receives formal and searching student evaluation. Curriculum, although entirely conventional as to student work requirement and class contact time, has been completely redesigned. As an aside, absolutely no credit is given for prior experience. No other types of students are permitted in the classes so that instruction can be targeted to experienced practitioners. Some things are speeded up much more than would be usual; some are stretched out. Discussions much more frequently involve critique of fundamental paradigms and assumptions than most faculty are accustomed to. Those faculty who survive find such teaching addictive. The program runs twelve months of the year. It took a decade to evolve.

Perhaps no particular generalization can be drawn from this example, but it does illustrate the assertion that quality education in new modes, for different clients, is complex and expensive if it is to be highly effective. Experiences with such innovations need to be shared more widely, so that quality institutions can provide alternatives to the questionable innovative program in lower-quality universities— programs that were initially developed to fill the vacuum created by mainline institutions.

Structural Disincentives. Some of the most difficult barriers to the redesign of programs come from university structures. They almost defy modification. Implicit recognition of them undoubtedly inhibits greatly the ability to focus on program design.

The first such structure is the manner in which universities have locked in their faculty to a pattern of specialization with an elaborate and pervasive tenure system. Changes in this system are probably impossible in the short run. But it should be noted that, if almost all program flexibility has been traded for tenure, a very high price indeed has been paid. It is important to note also that such a choice is not at all common in other innovative institutions in the society. The problem is not at all with tenure guarantees of academic freedom but rather with tenure's provision of guaranteed continuity of employment except for dismissal for cause or major financial exigency. In a time requiring simultaneous retrenchment and new program development, faculty staffing changes may be necessary. A more complex set of accepted options for closing programs as well as of incentives and requirements for faculty retraining and redeployment is badly needed.

Another structural attribute that poses a barrier to program redesign is our undifferentiated commitment to participative decision making. This is a very complex and subtle matter, but one that, in theory, is not quite as hopeless as the tenure issue. It is subtle and complex because there are times and situations in which participative decision making is the best way to produce improvement, but it is not entirely hopeless, in part, because such decision making already creates considerable frustration within the faculty itself—for example, with the current way of approaching change.

The problem with an uncritical and undifferentiated use of participative decision making is that it is too easy to surrender to interests lodged in the past. When the personal employment security of a tenure system is added to participative and parliamentary-like decision making, a powerful force for the preservation of the status quo is formed. New faculty in new areas are not hired as yet and hence cannot enter a coalition. Even the changes necessary for small redesign can be difficult. New mechanisms are needed beyond the typical standing committee and plenary faculty structures to bring the faculty voice to decision making.

Steps Leading to Solutions

Having noted these problems in developing new approaches in graduate education, we must ask what might be done to meet the new situation. There is insufficient space here to delineate solutions; in fact, many of them are not as yet known and will evolve only as a result of trial and error. But a few things can be noted.

In the first place, some attitudinal changes on the part of faculty and administration would be very helpful. Principally, it is time to stop decrying what is taking place and to embrace the future with its needs and opportunities. It would be desirable all around to move from a defensive static posture to a more aggressive, forward-looking one. Typically, persons shrink from this because change usually involves doing things that arouse apprehension or are to some degree distasteful. Change rearranges power relationships, for example, at times creating new winners and losers. But to do nothing also arouses apprehension and distaste and, furthermore, does not result in the solution of problems. It is actually dangerous, for instance, to project into the future as an inevitable necessity those educational arrangements that happen to have grown up over recent decades.

Secondly, making some changes in organizational forms and procedures should be considered. These changes should revolve around the issue of program design and how to improve it. Since such changes at this time cannot be made with an abundance of new resources, they will require various combinations, recombinations, and rearrangements. For example, matrix formulations that permit temporary organizational forms to arise to meet new needs often can be used in education to try out new ideas. A careful look at what educational technology may have in store in order to improve effectiveness, to increase the outreach, and to lower the costs of graduate education is highly desirable. It will not be possible to afford many changes if it is assumed that quality can be brought about only with increased costs and thereby with increased negative productivity, to borrow the economists' quaint phrase. An examination and softening of the traditional barriers that we built into organizational life (such as those between doctoral and master's programs, between academic and applied disciplines, and between traditional graduate and professional education) is needed. Many of these barriers are out of date and inhibit a successful institutional response to the need for change.

Much of the malaise in current graduate education results from a focus on the decline in resources, in the availablity of conventional careers for graduates, and, hence, in the availability of talented students. This malaise will only decrease when the new conditions are accepted and there is a move toward meeting them with relevant approaches. Attempts to do so, even though they will not all be successful, should do a great deal to reinvigorate and rejuvenate graduate education. University faculty and administrators see this need clearly when they evaluate other institutions in society; they now must include the university itself in that perception.

Paul A. Albrecht is executive vice-president of Claremont University Center and executive dean of the Claremont Graduate School. He is former chairman of the board of the Council of Graduate Schools in the United States, former president of the Western Association of Graduate Schools, and current member of the Senior Accrediting Commission, Western Association of Schools and Colleges.

Market forces suggest that this should be a period of extensive innovation in graduate education, but the importance of relative prestige to universities mutes incentives to innovate.

A Theory of Innovation in Graduate Education

Lewis C. Solmon

Prior to the mid 1960s, college graduation was an infrequent enough occurrence that those who completed college were still members of a national elite. College graduates were "special," and employers seeking highly talented employees drew from the pool of college graduates. By the late 1970s, open access to many colleges, as well as changing and sometimes lowered standards, led to the general view that there was nothing too special about merely graduating. Employers changed their "screening procedures" from emphasis on a college degree to the quality of college attended, grades earned, and major field. In some instances, years of attendance (that is, degree level) also became a hiring criterion, with master's and doctorate degree recipients being sought where bachelor's formerly sufficed.

But even these more stringent standards have been thrown into question as institutional quality has been redefined, grades have become inflated, and postbaccalaureate degree recipients have proliferated. In essence, with the possible exceptions of graduates from a few undersubscribed major fields and from a small number of ultraelite institutions, getting more education no longer assures people of "good" jobs (or of any jobs at all in some cases).

M. J. Pelczar, L. C. Solmon (Eds.). *Keeping Graduate Programs Responsive to National Needs.*
New Directions for Higher Education, no. 46. San Francisco: Jossey-Bass, June 1984.

At the same time as the colleges and universities of this country have had to face the consequences of their reduced standards and expanded output, they have been hit by the double whammy of a precipitous drop in the size of the college-going age cohort and of reduced funding. The latter derives from a prolonged serious recession, successful tax-reduction movements, and a general antipathy in the nation to governmental involvement and public expenditures combined with the increased questioning of the value of college. One way or another, institutions of higher learning need the financial resources that accompany student enrollments (either through tuition or through state aid based upon enrollments). Now there are fewer potential students to go around and those considering college or graduate school are having serious second thoughts, primarily because advanced learning no longer is the certain ticket to later economic success.

This scenario seems to imply that most institutions of higher education would have very strong incentives to offer an education that would give *their* students a competitive advantage in the labor market. Surely, to seek out new clients (such as adults or foreigners) or to embark upon dramatic fund-raising programs might help somewhat, but, without a steady flow of traditional students, most institutions will find themselves in desperate trouble. And the many elusive students will be those most concerned about jobs after graduation.

Thus, the basic hypothesis underlying this volume is that we should be able to observe a great deal of innovation in higher education as colleges and universities seek to prepare students better for the job market they will enter. The task is to identify types and patterns of innovation at both the undergraduate and graduate level. But there is now emerging a serious debate about how much innovation has actually occurred in higher education and about whether or not and where change might occur in the future. In part, this debate results from a lack of consensus on the meaning of innovation: Some observe that higher education has undergone tremendous changes over the past quarter century; others look at the same group of institutions and conclude that they are pretty much the same as they were twenty-five years ago. This difference in perception seems to be due to the fact that many things may or may not be classiffied as innovative, depending upon one's purpose and definition.

The Meaning of Innovation

Basically, innovations in higher education can be put into one of two general categories. The first is *process* innovation or administrative innovation. Into this category fall procedural changes, such as new forms of organization, joint operations between graduate schools and schools of continuing education, flexible scheduling, counseling programs, external degrees, self-directed study, job internship programs, co-op programs, outreach activities to the community, creative placement efforts, and so on. Marketing efforts, the search for new clients, and recruitment and retention efforts also belong in this category. In general, process innovations are ones that (1) do not alter the substance of the education offered, (2) are the prime responsibility of administrators rather than faculty, and so (3) do not impinge upon the demands on or prerogatives of ladder faculty. Basically, a strong, enlightened administration can achieve a substantial amount of process innovation.

The second category of innovation might be called *content* innovation or curricular innovation. Here we are talking about new disciplines, or programs, new kinds of scholars, new alliances among old disciplines, and new ideas. Content may be changed by stressing marketable skills that already may be provided but are not stressed, by radically altering curricula to provide such skills, by merely relabeling existing programs to stress new objectives, by merging weak programs with strong ones, or by developing separate, supplemental programs to compensate for deficiences in primary fields (for example, careers-in-business programs for humanities graduates). New uses of media, computers, and other instructional technology are types of content innovation. These are changes in the substance of the education offered.

Content innovations are ones that significantly affect the situation of ladder faculty by (1) causing the faculty to change what they do, (2) changing the reward structure or criteria for hiring, paying, and promoting faculty, and (3) in general imposing extra time and money costs on the entrenched faculty. Although some content changes may be mandated or imposed upon faculty, departments, or institutions, they require substantially more involvement of and cooperation by faculty than do process innovations. As we shall see in the section that follows, incentives for such change vary according to a faculty member's security, status, and field.

A Model

Our predictions of university (and program, administration, and faculty) behavior can be informed by obervations about how private corporations innovate. Basically, in the for-profit sector, once a new product or process (an invention) is identified the decision about whether or not to implement or introduce it (to create an innovation) is based upon potential *profitability*. In the private sector, increased profits are good for all groups with interests in the corporation (shareholders, managers, and employees). The benefits include increased viability, greater asset value, and usually higher salaries and greater job security for both managers and workers. Of course, labor-saving innovations might reduce the total number of employees, but the question of whether the introduction of more technology (machines) utlimately results in more or fewer jobs appears to be as yet unresolved. It is probably the case that the nature of jobs will change to some degree as the nonlabor inputs into the production process are modified. Nevertheless, for our purposes, let us assume that the innovation decision in the corporate sector is based upon probability estimates of the costs and benefits of such innovations, upon discounting of future impacts, and, in sum, upon profitability.

When we move to the university sector, certain differences are immediately apparent. First, the precondition for innovation, namely successful invention, may not be apparent. The actors in the university sector simply might not know what to do or what will work. Whereas a corporation may well know what a new type of machine will do before it decides whether or not to introduce it, a university probably does not know what the effects of, say, a new curriculum will be before it is introduced. Both Brown University and Stanford University have recently made substantial curricular revisions that initially appeared to be successful but were soon abandoned (Levine, 1978). In the university sector, the problem of accurately estimating potential costs and potential benefits is greater because there are fewer possibilities for controlled experiments with potential innovations. The risks of innovating are typically greater.

The second difference between the university and the corporate sectors is the fact that universities are not profit-seeking entities, and so the impact of any change in net benefits cannot be assessed as directly as can be done for private companies. Is there any analogy in the university sector to profits in the business sector? Garvin (1980), Breneman (1970), and Solmon (1976) have argued that institutional prestige of universities or departments is analogous to corporate profits. Prestige appears to bring benefits to most or all of the claimants to the outputs of universities: students, faculty, administrators, and the broader society. As prestige increases, so do the number and quality of applications to enroll, research grants, other government funding, private giving, the ability to recruit quality faculty, and so on.

This bears directly upon a third type of distinction between the corporate and university sectors. Although virtually any private corporation has the prospect of increasing profits, there are many colleges that rank so low in the status or prestige hierarchy that their prospects for increasing their prestige to a "respectable" level are virtually nil. Almost nothing they realistically can do can turn them into prestigious (or even measurably more prestigious) institutions. Whereas a buggy-whip producer can redirect the company's capital and labor to produce leather belts, a university does not have the flexibility to become much other than a university.

Therefore, prestige is not completely analogous to profits, and so other goals may have to be specified. Some of these, like revenue maximization or, ultimately, survival, may conflict with the goal of prestige maximization. And, just as university goals may conflict, so might the interests of the various claimants to the benefits of the university.

Conflicts of interest in outcomes are different when survival is at stake than when survival is taken for granted and prestige or revenue maximization is sought. Those whose jobs are secured by tenure have different incentives than do those faculty and administrators without tenure. Those who could benefit from outside resources (perhaps from research grants) have different interests than those who have few or no prospects in this area. Those who have alternative employment opportunities, either in the corporate or consulting worlds or at other universities, differ from those without other options. Those in "strong" fields (such as computer science) have different interests from those in "weak" fields (such as Latin). Those whose strength is in teaching undergraduates may seek different objectives than those whose comparative advantage is in research and the training of graduate students.

These conflicts make it extremely difficult in a university setting to achieve a consensus about the ultimate payoff to any innovation. Not only is its outcome uncertain but also the value of an agreed-upon outcome may be different depending upon where one sits.

Finally, the relationship between any innovation of the type focused upon here and the consensus goal is different in the corporate and the university sectors. In private corporations, the expected relationship between innovation and profits is positive; that is, when an innovation is attempted, the expectation is that profits will rise.

In the university sector, almost by definition, many innovations will necessarily lead to *reduced* prestige. In a very basic sense, prestige depends upon how closely a particular institution (or department) resembles Harvard, Berkeley, or Amherst (or the corresponding department there). Any innovation that results in greater differentiation from the most prestigious institutions will probably result in a decline in prestige (unless prestige is already so low that it cannot decline). Thus, moves toward vocationalism, new types of students, or new organizational arrangements will be viewed by those inside and outside of an institution as a sign of weakness and a lessening of prestige. Only those changes that *follow* the prestige leaders (recent examples include Harvard's new general education requirements and careers-in-business programs that retool and place humanities Ph.D.s) will be viewed positively.

The problem with such a "prestige leader" model is that the objectives of the most prestigious universities may differ from the less prestigious ones, or the interest groups in power may differ across institutions of different prestige levels. And what will work for Harvard (given the high quality of students and faculty and the strong financial base) simply may not work at a very low-prestige college. The most prestigious institutions may not be the appropriate role models for the lest prestigious ones (in regard to what will work), but the most prestigious institutions provide the criteria by which most other institutions will be judged.

Predictions

This discussion leads then to a number of predictions about the prospects for innovation in colleges and universities:

1. The most prestigious institutions will have little incentive to innovate. In the first place, they are already at the top of the prestige hierarchy, which is a relative scale, and so they cannot move up much. Second, these institutions do not face declining numbers of applicants or enrollments, since the payoff for students to attend a more prestigious institution is now greater than ever. Third, one function perceived by the leading departments in each field is to maintain its field of discipline, to preserve and extend knowledge as it is now known, and so not to take radical departures from what has been successful for them in the past.

2. Those innovations that do occur at the most prestigious institutions or departments will reflect (1) scientific or scholarly breakthroughs, combining with new perceived needs of society, or (2) special interests of powerful groups in the institu-

tion. Into the first category fall many of the new joint programs between strong disciplines (joint business-computer or business-science programs). In the second, we might place new auspices for conducting research (university-related genetic engineering firms to satisfy faculty desires to benefit from their research) or general education, more language requirements, and careers-in-business programs at Harvard and elsewhere (which, at least in part, serve to maintain enrollments in fields of declining interest for powerful faculty in the humanities).

3. In most cases, attempts by low-prestige departments to replicate innovations accomplished by the more prestigious ones will fail.

4. The medium-level prestige institutions are in the most difficult position. Since their existence is not threatened, the need to change in order to survive does not exist. Since most departments are more highly tenured than ever, faculty will perceive costs of change to be much greater than the benefits. Rewards are currently based upon publications, not curricular innovation. And any deviations from the "Harvard model" will run the risk of reducing prestige. Since every institution of even modest quality seeks to become "number one," this inertia extends from the top to the middle-level institutions.

5. Most innovations will occur in institutions or departments where prestige is already so low that deviation from the "Harvard model" will not significantly lower prestige. This innovation will take the form of changes in existing programs or of adding new programs, rather than in merging programs. Joint programs may be viewed by each department as "zero-sum game" where, if one group gains, the other loses. These innovations will be not-too-subtle attempts to attract new students in order to survive, rather than to increase prestige. Many will be merely window dressing and marketing ploys rather than substantive changes.

6. Much innovation will be initiated by administrators rather than faculty. Administrators may not have job security and so are more concerned with institutional survival than are faculty. They can make across-department decisions, whereas faculty generally focus on the single department where their interests and rewards lie.

Using a Cost-Benefit Analysis to Encourage Innovation

Space does not permit the presentation of details, but virtually all of the proposed hypotheses seem to be consistent with the data. Suffice it to say that the data that do exist seem to confirm that whatever innovation does occur, takes place primarily in the lowest-prestige colleges and universities. This is to be expected because in such institutions enrollment drops are most severe, chances of significantly improving or hurting prestige are slim, and faculty can focus upon curricular changes without much cost since research productivity is not a major criteria for promotion or pay increases.

However, the limited and narrow range of innovation accomplished by leading role-model institutions is unfortunate. Middle-level universities are discouraged from effective change. And the lowest-status ones might not be getting sufficient guidance.

A cost-benefit analysis framework can be used to categorize suggestions for successful innovation in colleges and universities. From it, the following points should be considered:

1. Expand the planning horizon to take account of long-term as well as short-term costs and benefits. Be willing to take certain risks; that is, do not require that success or benefits be known to a certainty before innovating. Recognize that a small chance of a large benefit may be worth as much as a certain but small payoff. Do not wait until the situation becomes desperate, when the evaluation of costs, benefits, and risks may become distorted. And remember that various claimants to the benefits of university activities may have different interests.

2. Remember that those people who potentially might be the best innovators do not have automatically the incentive to do so from the point of view of their own self-interest. Thus, explicit efforts must be made (and incentives provided) to get the best people thinking about the problems. The natural inclination is to have those with the lowest opportunity costs gravitate toward new problems, but they might not be the best people to do so. One source of new ideas is "new blood" on the campus; thus, programs that encourage expansion or turnover of staff and faculty should help with innovation. (John Silber, president of Boston University, is viewed by many as a major innovator—or at least one who shakes up whatever institution he serves. It is rumored that, when he was interviewing for the B.U. presidency, the first question he asked was, "Whom can I fire?") But unless the criteria for promotion, tenure, and pay increases are changed to reward innovative activity (rather than using research as the only criterion), even new people will

not help. In particular, interdepartmental cooperation must be implemented without placing participating faculty in "double jeopardy," whereby to be rewarded they must satisfy the standards of several departments. This situation simply increases the costs to the faculty who participate in innovative activities. The responsibility for new curriculum development or faculty involvement should be given to one department or none will take responsibility.

3. Because of differences in perceived payoffs and costs, observers generally assume that much of the significant innovation will be at the instigation of administrators rather than faculty. On the other hand, innovations imposed by administrative fiat without faculty consent are almost certainly destined to fail, particularly those that require faculty cooperation. Administrators must have strong authority, but also they must have faculty support and flexibility in order to reallocate certain resources. And, apparently, innovation is more successful in more simplified, less bureaucratic, less formal, decentralized, less stratified, and more flexible organizations. All of these characteristics reduce the costs of administrative action. Innovations will fail if their introduction or implementation places undue and unrewarded burdens on either administrators or faculty.

4. Any or all changes are not necessarily desirable. Thus, universities should not innovate just to change. Before making major changes, an institution should attempt to explicate its goals. Then the decision must be made as to whether proposed changes are compatible with accepted goals or whether new goals are to be established. In many cases, when goals are changed, institutions lose their identity and thereby are worse off than if no change had been made. In most cases, innovation will seek new ways to satisfy goals consistent with the existing university mission. Within that mission, questions might be asked about how to differentiate the product of the particular university and about what services can be provided to the local and national communities that will increase demand.

5. Most successful innovations in higher education are marginal or incremental, rather than holistic. Basically, successful innovation will supplement existing programs rather than throw old ones out. Innovative enclaves will develop within existing organizations; perhaps after identifying role models, faculty and administrators will form experimental subunits. Radical changes usually present unacceptable risks. It must also be recognized that content (curricular) innovation may require process innovation to support it. A new program aimed at older, part-time students will fail if it is offered during

working hours. Yet it is surprising how many faculty are reluctant to vary their teaching schedules to accomodate sought-after new clients. Clear in such cases, costs are viewed as exceeding benefits.

6. In graduate education, the concept of marginal change implies that most successful innovations will parallel the encouragement of strong graduate programs in the traditional sense, rather than the replacement of them with new programs. In the latter case, new programs not only will pose a threat but also will be subject to criticism that they are merely cosmetic marketing ploys unsupported by academic credibility. But it must also be remembered that both basic and applied graduate programs can be academically respectable.

Some of these points are general and their relevance to cost-benefit analysis indirect. But, hopefully, they can serve as guidelines, and they can stimulate discussion as innovations are considered by universities.

References

Breneman, D. W. *An Economic Theorty of Ph.D. Production: The Case at Berkeley.* Berkeley: Office of the Vice-President—Planning, University of California, 1970.

Garvin, D. A. *The Economics of University Behavior.* New York: Academic Press, 1980.

Levine, A. "The Life and Death of Innovation in Higher Education." Occasional Papers Series no. 2. Buffalo: Department of Higher Education, State University of New York, 1978.

Solmon, L. C. *Male and Female Graduate Students: The Question of Equal Opportunity.* New York: Praeger, 1976.

Lewis C. Solmon is associate dean and professor in the Graduate School of Education, University of California, Los Angeles.

There is evidence both for and against the proposition that innovation is punished by surveys that rank academic quality.

Innovation in Ph.D. Programs and Scores in Reputational Rankings

David S. Webster

It is frequently said that academic departments whose professors are innovative in the topics they investigate in their research, in the subjects they cover in their teaching, in the methods they use in both their research and teaching, or in some combination of these areas are rated lower than they deserve to be in "reputational" rankings of universities. Many of the raters, so this argument goes, teach at the highest-ranked departments in their disciplines, the ones that set the norm for all others, and they punish "maverick" departments by rating them lower than they should be rated.

I am grateful to Robert Lucid, chairman of the English Department at the University of Pennsylvania, for information about English departments, and to Susan Watkins, assistant professor of sociology at the University of Pennsylvania, for information about sociology departments. Any errors of fact or interpretation that remain are my responsibility alone. I am also grateful to William Korn, programmer at the Higher Education Research Institute, Los Angeles, for sending me printouts of the data from the National Academy of Sciences' 1982 academic quality rankings and to Ruth Ebert, secretary at the University of Pennsylvania's Graduate School of Education, for her editorial and clerical help.

M. J. Pelczar, L. C. Solmon (Eds.). *Keeping Graduate Programs Responsive to National Needs.*
New Directions for Higher Education, no. 46. San Francisco: Jossey-Bass, June 1984.

31

This argument has appeared in print many times. For example, William Arrowsmith (1976), the distinguished classics scholar, wrote in the preface of W. Patrick Dolan's *The Ranking Game* that the effect of reputational rankings is "to reduce diversity, to reward conformity or respectability, to penalize genuine experiment or risk. There is, also, I believe, an obvious tendency to promote the prevalence of disciplinary dogma and orthodoxy" (p. ix).

Elsewhere in the book, Dolan (1976) said of reputational rankings, such as those done by Cartter (1966) and by Roose and Andersen (1970), "First, the large, orthodox academic departments are rewarded, and bring prestige to their universities. If an academic department, for whatever reason, had decided to concentrate strength in certain areas and not build in the orthodox fashion, it would suffer. . . . The university would realize it had been penalized for experimentation" (p. 36).

After the publication of the multidimensional ranking by the National Academy of Sciences (NAS — Jones and others, 1982), a distinguished physicist explained his department's faculty's below-average reputational ranking for scholarly quality with a similar line of reasoning (Seifert, 1983a):

> "The ratings tended to slight smaller departments, particularly those with uncommon specialities," said James Van Allen, chairman of the [University of Iowa] physics and astronomy department. . . . "Further, the U.I. department's research specialty is space physics, a relatively uncommon activity in most physics departments," Van Allen said.
>
> For that reason, he said, "our work is not well known among comparable physics departments around the country." [p. 3-A].

Evidence That Innovation Is Punished

Those who argue that innovation and experimentation are not rewarded in academic quality rankings have some persuasive evidence on their side. For example, the seven major, multidisciplinary reputational rankings, from the first one by Raymond Hughes (1925) to the recent one by the NAS, generally rate only those disciplines in which substantial numbers of Ph.D.s have been conferred nationally in recent years. So, if an institution is innovative enough to establish doctorate-granting programs in disciplines in which relatively few students earn doctorates, such as the departments of rhetoric and of Scandinavian at the University of California (UC) Berkeley, of Celtic languages and literature at Harvard, of folklore and folk life at the University of Pennsylvania, and the School of Near Eastern and Judaic Studies at Brandeis, it will not get any "credit" for these departments in reputational rankings.

Similarly, if a university is innovative enough to establish interdisciplinary programs, it will not get "credit" for them either, since the major reputational rankings do not cover them. While one would not expect such an esoteric interdisciplinary Ph.D. program as the one in Buddhist studies at UC-Berkeley to be covered by these rankings, such less esoteric and academically outstanding programs as those in social thought at the University of Chicago, East Asian languages at Columbia University, and history and sociology of science at the University of Pennsylvania have never been included in a multidisciplinary academic quality ranking.

Another argument that supports the position that innovation is not rewarded in academic quality rankings is the extraordinary stability of the highest-ranked departments and universities, over many years, in these rankings. Once a department or institution reaches the highest levels, it seldom falls too far, leaving very few spots at the top open to which others can ascend.

For example, in Figure 1 are two lists. On the left are the fifteen highest-ranked universities, overall in Hughes' (1925) reputational

Figure 1. The Fifteen Highest-Ranked Institutions in Two Reputational Rankings

Hughes (1925)

1. University of Chicago
2. Harvard University
3. Columbia University
4. Yale University
5. University of Wisconsin
6. Princeton University
7. Johns Hopkins University
8. University of Michigan
9. University of California-Berkeley
10. Cornell University
11. University of Illinois-Urbana
12. University of Pennsylvania
13. University of Minnesota
14. Stanford University
15. Ohio State University

NAS (1982)

1. Massachusetts Institute of Technology
2. Harvard University
3. University of California-Berkeley
4. California Institute of Technology
5. Stanford University
6. Princeton University
6. Yale University
8. University of Chicago
9. University of California-Los Angeles
10. Columbia University
10. University of Michigan
12. Cornell University
13. University of Wisconsin
14. University of Illinois
15. University of Pennsylvania

ranking. On the right are the fifteen highest-ranked universities in the NAS ranking (Jones and others, 1982). Since neither Hughes nor the NAS aggregated their discipline-by-discipline scores into institution-wide ones, we have compiled these lists in the following manner. Hughes asked his judges to rate each of twenty departments from one to five according to their quality of graduate work. He then ranked them by multiplying their "one" ratings by four, their "two" ratings by three, their "three" ratings by two, and their "four" and "five" ratings by one. We added his scores for each department to get institution-wide totals.

For the NAS rankings, we took the mean score of all the programs that were included. Thus, since only those programs that the NAS rated contribute to an institution's score, universities are not penalized when they have no Ph.D. program in a discipline. This method clearly favors institutions such as the Massachusetts Institute of Technology (MIT) and the California Institute of Technology (Caltech), which, while not having across-the-board offerings, are outstanding in those programs they do offer. Nonetheless, it probably presents a reasonably good assessment of the fifteen best institutions for doctoral training in America. We have omitted two institutions, although their mean scores were high enough to place them among the top fifteen, because these scores were based on only a handful of programs. They are Rockefeller University (five programs) and the University of California-San Francisco (three programs).

In any case, Figure 1 shows the remarkable similarity between these two lists of America's fifteen highest-ranked universities, based on reputational rankings published forty-seven years apart. Twelve of the fifteen schools on each list are identical. Even the three institutions on each list that fail to appear on the other do not fall very far below the top fifteen: Johns Hopkins, the University of Minnesota, and Ohio State University, which were seventh, thirteenth, and fifteenth on the 1925 list, by 1982 fell, respectively, to tied for twenty-seventh, tied for twenty-third, and forty-second. Thus they all still ranked quite high among the 228 doctorate-granting universities covered by the NAS.

On the schools listed in 1982 but not 1925, MIT, ranked first in 1982, had been nineteenth in Hughes's reputational ranking; Caltech, fourth in 1982, had been eighteenth; only U.C.L.A., ninth in 1982, had not been listed by Hughes (and it was established in 1919, only a few years before he published his ranking).

This stability in the positions of the highest-ranked institutions supports those who argue that innovation fails to be rewarded in reputational rankings. There is little or no reason to believe that the top-ranked institutions, or individual departments and programs at them, are necessarily the most innovative ones, and thus the fact that the same, probably not especially innovative, universities remain at the top continually for decades strongly suggests that their programs and departments are ranked highly for qualities other than their innovativeness. (For evidence that the same institutions that were ranked at the top of the reputational rankings in 1925 and 1982 were also, by and large, ranked at the top of all the multidisciplinary reputational rankings done between those years, see Webster, 1983.)

Evidence That Innovation Is Not Punished

On the other hand, there is reason to think that innovation is *not* penalized in reputational rankings. The NAS ranking asked raters to judge programs according not only to their faculty's scholarly quality but also to the raters' own familiarity with these programs. The correlation between the reputation of a program's faculty for scholarly quality and the rater's familiarity with that program was .96 for disciplines in the mathematical and physical sciences (Grimes, 1982) and about the same for disciplines in other fields.

It seems likely, in the absence of evidence to the contrary and notwithstanding the opinion of James Van Allen quoted earlier, that innovative departments may be better known by others in the discipline than mainstream departments of about equal quality. Instead of being merely one of a group of mainstream departments, they stand out by doing something that few or no other departments do, just as entire institutions that are outside the mainstream, like Bob Jones University, Bennington College, Antioch College, Berea College, and Evergreen State College often are better known than more orthodox institutions of no less academic quality.

If, indeed, raters are more familiar with innovative departments and programs than with others of equivalent quality, as seems plausible, and since in the NAS ranking "familiarity" and reputation for faculty's scholarly quality correlated at about .96 for most departments, then being innovative should *help* a department's rating, not hurt it.

In addition, it is clear that some departments have managed to remain outside the mainstream of their discipline over many years and still be rated high, in some cases very high, in reputational rankings. Yale Law School, for example, for years has incorporated into its curriculum the "findings, concepts, and suggestions of the social sciences" (*Yale Law School Bulletin*, 1978, p. 19), much more so than most other law schools. One of its recent catalogues is liberally sprinkled with listings of such courses as "Anthropology of Law," "Political and Civil Rights," "Sociology of Law: Introduction," and "Psychoanalysis and Law." It even offers a course in "Philosophy and Law" and another on two contemporary philosophers, John Rawls and Robert Nozick. Yet despite this unconventional curriculum, all three multidisciplinary ratings of professional schools conducted since 1973 have ranked Yale as the nation's second-best law school, behind Harvard (Margulies and Blau, 1973, Blau and Margulies, 1974–75, Cartter, 1977). On the other hand, since Yale Law School does not grant Ph.D.s, we must be cautious in generalizing from its success in reputational rankings to that of the Ph.D. programs that are the main subject of this chapter.

As another example, the University of California at Los Angeles's sociology department is less quantitative and positivistic than most other sociology departments at major universities. Some of its leading figures are the theorist Jeffrey Alexander, the ethnomethodologist Harold Garfinkel, and the conversational analyst Emanuel Schegloff. Yet in the NAS ranking its faculty was rated ninth in the United States in reputation for scholarly quality.

There is abundant evidence, too, from the discipline of English that maverick departments can be rated quite high in reputational rankings. In the 1950s, the University of Chicago's department was well known for its several eminent faculty members, including R. S. Crane, Elder Olson, and Norman Maclean, who analyzed literary texts according to Aristotelian principles. While there is some question about whether an approach more than 2,000 years can properly be called "innovative," Chicago's English department certainly was widely considered to be different from mainstream English departments then, its approach to literature even being savagely satirized in Frederick Crews's *Pooh Perplex* (Penwiper, 1963). Yet in a reputational ranking published in 1959 (Keniston, 1959), Chicago's English department was ranked eighth in the United States "on the basis of the quality of [its] faculty as scholars" (p. 115).

There are many other examples of English departments outside the mainstream of the discipline doing well in reputational rankings. The University of Iowa's department has long been one of the few that allows Ph.D. candidates to specialize in creative writing; it even accepts "imaginative writing" as Ph.D. dissertations. Yet of twenty-one departments at Iowa that were judged for faculty's scholarly reputation in the NAS rankings, English earned a standard score of fifty-seven, with sixty the mean and a standard deviation of ten. This score tied English for the second highest of the twenty-one of University of Iowa programs that were rated (Seifert, 1983b).

The English department at the State University of New York (SUNY)-Buffalo is another unorthodox one. For one thing, it eschews the very broad *"Beowulf* to Virginia Woolf" coverage that is commonplace in America's leading doctorate-granting English departments and concentrates, more than most, on modern authors. For another, it probably has more professors than any other English department, including Norman Holland, Robert Rogers, Murray Schwartz, and Mark Schechner, who engage in the controversial practice of using psychoanalytic theories to analyze literary texts. Still, in the NAS rankings it achieved a standard score for scholarly reputation of sixty, far highest than any other humanities program at SUNY-Buffalo.

The University of California at Irvine department of English and comparative literature is still another department that is outside the mainstream. Under the leadership of University Professor Murray Krieger, it concentrates, both in research and teaching, more on critical theory than does any other major English department. Yet in the NAS study it achieved a standard score of fifty-seven for this faculty's scholarly reputation, higher than any of the other four humanities programs in which UC-Irvine was rated.

The Need for Systematic Study

This chapter is a first attempt to explore the question of whether innovative, unorthodox, outside-the-mainstream departments are penalized in reputational rankings of universities, but the matter needs to be studied systematically. Several factors should be taken into account, including the following.

First, what is an "innovative" department? Can one that uses principles of analyzing literary texts dating back to Aristotle be called "innovative"? For that matter, can the University of Iowa's English department, which, while it has been unusually hospitable to creative writing, nonetheless has remained quite traditional in other respects, properly be called an innovative department? Perhaps it should be considered a basically traditional department that has one innovative feature.

Another question is how to deal with innovations that are picked up and used by many other institutions. For example, Christopher Langdell's (Malone, 1933) case method of studying law, which he introduced at Harvard in the 1870s, spread rapidly to other law schools after one of Langdell's former students introduced it at Columbia in 1890. Such recent innovations as courses and programs in black studies and women's studies were introduced at hundreds of campuses within a few years after their inception, making them difficult or impossible to study as innovations at particular campuses (Riesman, 1977). Perhaps the best or most adaptable innovations are soon picked by up by other campuses, so that when we think we are studying innovations we are actually dealing with only the less successful or adaptable ones, the ones that failed to spread elsewhere.

In addition, the question of whether innovation is penalized in reputational rankings may too broadly framed. Very likely there are field differences. For example sociologists, according to studies of academicians, are more liberal politically than people in most other disciplines (Ladd and Lipset, 1975). They therefore may be more hospitable to innovation and less apt to penalize it in academic quality rankings than, say, art historians. Or perhaps their liberalism on national political issues does not extend to curricular innovation. There may well turn out to be differences even within disciplines. Historians, for example, may prove to be more hospitable to the apparent rigor and scientific basis of quantitative methods for studying history, the so-called cliometrics, than to the apparently fuzzier, less rigorous psychohistory. They may thus, in reputational rankings, "punish" history departments that feature the latter innovation but not punish those that feature the former.

We have frequently discussed departments that are widely considered innovative in their disciplines and then shown that these have been ranked highly in reputational rankings or that they have been ranked higher than other departments in the same area (such as the humanities). But that is hardly proof that these departments have not been "punished" for their differentness. It is possible that they would have been ranked even higher had they been more orthodox.

More questions have been raised here than answered. At least it should be obvious that the homily that reputational rankings of universities penalize innovative departments and programs needs to be tested. Systematic work is needed to show how, if at all, innovation, experimentation, and lack of orthodoxy in research and teaching affect Ph.D. programs' ratings in academic quality rankings.

References

Arrowsmith, W. A. "Preface." In W. P. Dolan, *The Ranking Game: The Power of the Academic Elite.* Lincoln: University of Nebraska Printing and Duplicating Service, 1976.
Blau, P. M., and Margulies, R. Z. "The Reputations of American Professional Schools." *Change,* 1974–75, *6* (10), 42–47.
Cartter, A. M. *An Assessment of Quality in Graduate Education.* Washington, D.C.: American Council on Education, 1966.

Cartter, A. M. "The Cartter Report on the Leading Schools of Education, Law, and Business." *Change,* 1977, *9* (2), 44–48.

Dolan, W. P. *The Ranking Game: The Power of the Academic Elite.* Lincoln: University of Nebraska Printing and Duplicating Service, 1976.

Grimes, R. N. "The Value and Purposes of Academic Ratings." *Chronicle of Higher Education,* 1982, *25* (10), 29.

Hughes, R. M. *A Study of Graduate Schools of America.* Oxford, Ohio: Miami University Press, 1925.

Jones, L. V., Lindzey, G., and Coggeshall, P. E. (Eds.). *An Assessment of Research-Doctorate Programs in the United States.* Washington, D.C.: National Academy Press, 1982.

Keniston, H. *Graduate Study and Research in the Arts and Sciences at the University of Pennsylvania.* Philadelphia: University of Pennsylvania Press, 1959.

Ladd, E. C., Jr., and Lipset, S. M. *The Divided Academy: Professors and Politics.* New York: McGraw-Hill, 1975.

Malone, D. (Ed.). *Dictionary of American Biography.* Vol. 10. New York: Scribner's, 1933.

Margulies, R. Z., and Blau, P. M. "America's Leading Professional Schools." *Change,* 1973, *5* (9), 21–27.

Penwiper, D. C. "A Complete Analysis of *Winnie-the-Pooh.*" In C. Crews, *The Pooh Perplex.* New York: Dutton, 1963.

Riesman, D. *Constraint and Variety in American Education.* Lincoln: University of Nebraska Press, 1977.

Roose, K. K., and Andersen, C. J. *A Rating of Graduate Programs.* Washington, D.C.: American Council on Education, 1970.

Seifert, C. "Many Department Chairmen Question Study's Value, Accuracy." *Iowa City Press-Citizen,* January 17, 1983a, p. 3-A.

Seifert, C. "Survey Gives U.I. Grad Programs a 'C'." *Iowa City Press-Citizen,* January 17, 1983, p. 3-A.

Webster, D. S. "America's Highest-Ranked Graduate Schools, 1925–1982." *Change,* 1983, *15* (4), 14–24.

Yale Law School Bulletin, 1978–79. New Haven, Conn.: Yale University, 1978, p. 19.

David S. Webster is assistant professor of higher education at the Graduate School of Education at the University of Pennsylvania.

Assessing the quality of graduate programs involves asking
how well students are enabled to achieve program objectives.

Assessing the Quality of Innovative Graduate Programs

Richard Millard

In order to deal effectively with the issue of quality assessment in innovative graduate programs, we need to have some fairly clear idea of what
we mean by "quality," of the range of "graduate education," and of what
constitutes "innovation." There frequently is less than agreement on the
meaning of any of these concepts: The debate over the nature and
definition of quality is about as old as the human species. Whenever
one tries to delimit the range of graduate education, one is likely to dis-
cover that the exceptions overwhelm the rule. And innovation is frequently in the eye of the beholder; to talk about it effectively at least
requires a date, a tradition, and a perspective.

Four Definitions of Quality

There are at least four definitions of quality that have been used
or assumed in relation to educational programs and institutions. The
first, in fact, is a nondefinition. It is the view that quality is an ineffable
characteristic of something, in this case education, that the something
either has or does not have. You recognize it when you see it but you
cannot define it. This is not very useful and tends to reduce quality to a

M. J. Pelczar, L. C. Solmon (Eds.). *Keeping Graduate Programs Responsive to National Needs.*
New Directions for Higher Education, no. 46. San Francisco: Jossey-Bass, June 1984.

matter of taste about which no standards are applicable except individual preference. If one is not so democratic as to admit everyone's taste, then it is essential to decide whose intuition or qualitative insight is correct, and the definition provides no help in such a decision.

The second definition relies on social consensus and takes the democratic aspects of the first definition seriously. In effect, it says that quality is what all people, or most people, or knowledgeable people agree upon. This does not get us very far beyond the first definition, for even if one restricts it to "knowledgeable people," such people do disagree, and the only appeal can be to a larger sample or a different group. In practice, this definition tends to become reliance either on tradition or on popularity vote. The reliance on knowledgeable people imbued with tradition was strikingly illustrated by the Yale faculty of 1828, which closed the curriculum for all times against the debilitating effects of modern languages and natural sciences. The popularity vote has been illustrated by more than one statistical survey that ranks academic departments. Such surveys may be fair indices of how well a department is known but may have little to do with the kind of education that takes place.

The third definition involves the use of a single paradigm to signify quality. This is essentially the Platonic idea of "the Good." Educational institutions or programs approximate its embodiment. The difficulty with this definition lies in the identification of this paradigm. In educational practice, the paradigm usually takes the form of a model of what constitutes the best college or university or school. The major problem with this is that it tends to do violence to the diversity of legitimate educational objectives and the institutions that embody them. Using this concept in quality assessment, one tends to look for the quantitative process characteristics of that "best" institution and apply them across the board regardless of other institutions' mission or circumstances. The result is likely to be educational homogenization, leaving us with leading institutions, copies of leading institutions, copies of copies of leading institutions, and so on — like the shadows in Plato's cave. This result disregards the appropriateness or even the possibility of excellence in institutions or programs of radically different types.

The fourth definition approaches quality contextually. It accepts the idea of paradigm but places the paradigm within the activity or object itself as involving its effectiveness according to type. Quality is thus "achievement in kind." The quality of a knife, for example, lies in its ability to cut what it is supposed to cut, and there are identifiable conditions or standards for assessing it in the light of its objective. The quality of an educational institution or program is a function of its effective utilization of resources to achieve appropriate educational objectives. Thus, an institution's norm is implicit within this definition, and its quality is determined by how well its various components cohere in achieving its educational objective or objectives. Faculty, students, resources, location or locations, and results or outcomes (including value added) are all relevant to the quality of the operation.

This perception of quality has the advantage of being relatively precise yet applicable to the variety of institutions and programs designed to meet the diverse legitimate educational needs of students and society. It is equally applicable to traditional and new or emerging programs and to a variety of forms of delivery. At first glance, it might seem to imply that standards for assuring quality must be unique to each program or institution. This, however, does not follow. It is possible to establish general standards for assessing the effective utilization of resources for the achievement of educationally appropriate objectives.

A Brief History of Quality Assessment in Education

Acceptance of the conception of quality as achievement in kind and of standards as the generalizable statements of the conditions of such achievement has not always characterized the accrediting community. The extent to which this concept is accepted today has been the result of an evolution, and, as is frequently the case with evolution, vestiges of older forms still remain and can be sources of tension within the academic and accrediting communities. Earlier standards tended to be much more closely related to the single-paradigm approach. These earlier standards were essentially prescriptive institutional or program characteristics, quantitatively reportable and process oriented, which defined what a "good" institution or program was. In most cases, these were input factors, and the operating norm was what the best institutions do. It was assumed that everyone knew which the "best" institutions were.

In the mid 1930s, a report prepared by the Committee on Revision of Standards for the North Central Association of Colleges and Schools prompted a major reassessment. Basically, it proposed that an institution should not be judged on the basis of a series of fixed characteristics but in terms of the purposes it seeks to serve and the total pattern it presents as an institution of higher education. Standards should be developed as conditions of an effective fulfillment of mission.

Within a relatively short period of time, this approach to accreditation and this conception of standards were adopted by the regional and national accrediting associations and gained considerable ground with professional or specialized accrediting bodies. For specialized accrediting associations, the program objectives involve not only the general institutional program objectives but also the more specific objectives related to preparing competent professionals in the field in question.

Given this evolution and acceptance of the conception of institutional program quality as effective utilization of resources to achieve appropriate educational objectives, we can see that the assessment of graduate programs, whether traditional or innovative, takes on somewhat different dimensions than are sometimes considered. For example, a critical question is not simply "what are the qualifications of the faculty?" (as important as these are) but "how effectively is the qualified faculty utilized to achieve the objectives of the program?"

Applying Quality Assessment to Graduate Education

Graduate education serves a wide variety of objectives: some disciplinary, some research-oriented, some interdisciplinary, some professional, some career entry, some career development, and all possible mixtures of the above. If this is the case, then the key to the definition of graduate programs, both by type and individually, is the specific set of objectives of the program or programs in question.

Further, the development of such objectives for each program is necessary before effective quality assessment of the program can even take place. Without a clear statement of the objectives of the program, quality assessment is likely to be either an exercise in nonrelevance, or an attempt to fit the program into a Procrustean bed based upon someone's grasp of the Platonic ideal with no regard for what the program is designed to do, or both. This is not to say that the objectives of scholarly or research activity or of professional proficiency in a particular field are or should be idiosyncratic to particular programs or institutions. These may and should be determined by scholars, researchers, professionals, educators, practitioners, and the requirements of the field in question. It is, however, to recognize that such objectives are multiple, not single, and that the particular combination of these that constitute the objectives of individual programs may vary legitimately. Accordingly, the effectiveness (and thus the quality) of the program should be assessed in the light of the unique objectives of that program.

Rating scales that fail to take into account unique program objectives at best are likely to be misleading and at worst can perpetrate major injustices to the programs in question. At the same time, an institution that calls its programs something they are not, where the programs' real or perceived objectives differ from the stated objectives, is misleading both its students and the public. Under such circumstances, not only such an institution's quality but also its integrity are questionable.

In addition to the variety of objectives of graduate education, there are obviously a variety of conditions for the achievement of such objectives. While resources, for example, do not guarantee quality, as is sometimes assumed, adequate resources for the achievement of the educational objectives are a necessary condition of quality. Thus, an institution with limited resources either should not be involved in graduate education or should choose very carefully the areas of graduate education where its resources can be utilized effectively to achieve the relevant objectives. This may pose serious problems for institutions with restricted or diminishing resources; they may have to choose whether to delete certain graduate programs or to shift other priorities and objectives to sustain the programs in question. To do neither is to sacrifice quality and lower the integrity of the institution.

Other factors that have a direct bearing on the achievement of objectives include the relevance of faculty qualifications, the availability of clinical and laboratory resources (where applicable), and the time and place commitments of the institution. An institution in a rural setting should think long and hard before undertaking a graduate program in urban studies. What an institution can legitimately do, the educational objectives it can obtain, and thus the types of graduate education, if any, it should be involved in are related to its resources, its size, its location, and the general environment in which it exists. This would seem to be a truism, and yet some of the marginal graduate programs now struggling for survival were established with more concern for institutional ambition than for environmental and resource realism.

Another factor of critical importance in the quality assessment of graduate programs is the relation of the objective or objectives of the programs to the overall objectives of the institution. Are the graduate programs an integral part of the total institutional mission, or are they add-ons for whatever reason—income, prestige, expediency, political pressure, and so on? That they are integral to the mission of major research universities or universities with a commitment to various forms of professional education may be clear. The addition of new graduate and professional programs to previously undergraduate institutions or to institutions with limited graduate offerings in fields not directly related to its undergraduate work clearly changes the character of the institution. The critical question is the extent to which such additions reflect a real change in commitment with appropriate allocation of resources. If they do not reflect such commitment, regardless of the objectives of the program, the probability that these objectives will be achieved is not very great.

But there is another side to these considerations: Institutions that establish graduate programs due to the external pressure of a professional group, or a particular clientele, or due to the temporary availability of special funding—programs that involve objectives not in harmony with the total institutional mission—may find not only their program support and quality in jeopardy but also that program continuance constitutes a threat to the integrity and quality of the institution itself.

Basically, then, the assessment of quality in graduate programs, like the assessment of the quality of educational programs in general, is a function of determining the extent to which resources are utilized effectively to achieve educationally appropriate objectives. If this is the case, then the relevant questions in such quality assessment are not simply what the level of support is, what the qualifications of the faculty are, what learning and library resources are available, and so on, but whether they are adequate and how they are utilized to achieve the program and institutional objectives or mission. The assessment process is clearly complicated by the variety of programs under the -graduate banner, but what this underlines is the essential need for clear and accurate statements of the objectives of each graduate program and of the institution's educational mission as it relates to the program in question. These are preconditions of any effective quality assessment whether it be through institutional program self-assessment or by institutional or specialized accrediting bodies.

Assessing Innovative Programs

When one deals specifically with the question of assessing the quality of innovative graduate programs, the critical question becomes what constitutes an "innovative program." If we can define "innovation," then the next question is whether the assessment of quality in such programs is generically different from quality assessment of graduate programs in general.

Today, when one talks about innovative programs in graduate education, one tends to be talking about programs beyond the baccalaureate level with unique objectives, or programs involving what are considered different modes of delivery, or both. In relation to objectives, one can always legitimately ask whether the objectives are appropriate to graduate education. However, with the wide variety of objectives of different graduate programs, this is not likely to delimit the field very extensively. To be a "graduate program," one can say that, in terms of content or learning objectives, it should be in fact postbaccalaureate in the field in question, although the line between upper-division undergraduate work and master's level graduate work at times is not only thin but wavy. Further, there are legitimate master's programs designed to introduce persons without undergraduate work in the particular field to the field in a focused or concentrated manner that builds upon the student's general background.

If the innovative program's objectives are within the scope of graduate education, a second quality issue is whether the objectives are relevant to the mission or objectives of the institution. Here the questions raised earlier of environmental realism and resources become crucial whether the program is innovative or traditional.

Even more crucial is the question of whether the mode of delivery or student involvement enables the student or students to attain the objectives. That there are alternate routes to most objectives may in fact be the case, but, in relation to certain types of educational objectives, there clearly are limiting conditions. One can hardly become a research scientist without access to laboratories or a clinical psychologist without clinical experience. Whether the program is research-oriented, practice-oriented, or some combination of these, there will be in most cases some limiting conditions on the mode of delivery or the nature of student involvement essential to attainment of the objectives. Under any circumstances, the matter of results or outcomes is important in determining whether the objectives have been or can be met. However, as the mode of delivery or the nature of student involvement varies progressively from what might be described as usual expectations, comparative results or outcomes both of "traditional" and of "innovative" routes to the objectives become critical.

While results are crucial, this is not to negate the importance of process, since it is the process that produces the results. Still, if the objectives are not attained, regardless of how intriguing the process may be, it is meaningless to talk about the quality of the program.

Innovation is or should be an integral part of all education. Because among other things, it is concerned with change, additions to knowledge, and preparation for changing professions, graduate education to be viable must be not only amenable to innovation but also a source of innovation. What is critically important is that we not confuse quality with tradition or rely on a conception of quality that entails tradition as part of the definition. The temptation to do so is particularly high in periods of crisis or when higher or graduate education is under attack as in some respects it is today. To confuse quality with tradition is to enshrine ossification. It is equally important, however, not to confuse quality with innovation. Both tradition and innovation are in themselves quality-neutral.

Thus, if the quality of educational programs or institutions is to be assessed in terms of effective utilization of resources to achieve appropriate academic objectives, then the assessment of innovative graduate programs is in fact no different from the assessment of traditional programs. What this underlines, however, is that the standards for assessment of quality for all programs cannot be simple quantitative requirements, but must be judgmental conditions related to achievement of the objectives. What is at issue is the integrity not only of the specific program or programs but also of the educational institution or organization itself in the achievement of its mission.

Reference

Zook, G. F., and Haggerty, M. E. (Eds.). *The Evaluation of Higher Institutions,* Vol. 1, *Principles of Accrediting Higher Institutions.* Chicago: University of Chicago Press, 1936.

Richard Millard is president of the Council on Postsecondary Accreditation.

The humanities have informally initiated a four-part strategy to deal with the shortage of jobs for individuals with graduate credentials.

Diversity in the Humanities: Blending the Old and the New

Richard D. Fulton

The humanities today seem to be sailing somewhere between Scylla and Charybdis. On one side are those who recognize that traditional humanistic concerns in graduate education and research must continue to be pursued, or the humanities will be destroyed. On the other are those who contend that traditional concerns are irrelevant in contemporary society, and, unless the humanities can begin training people for productive jobs, they should no longer be supported—in short, they should be destroyed.

Developing a Four-Part Strategy

Odysseus survived the passage between Scylla and Charybdis but suffered the loss of six of his companions. The humanities expect that through better strategic planning they may make their passage unscathed. Although the planning has not been formally coordinated among disciplines, it generally consists of the following parts:

First, humanities disciplines have continued to concentrate a major part of their effort in traditional areas of graduate study and research, producing research scholars in literature, history, philosophy, and so on.

M. J. Pelczar, L. C. Solmon (Eds.). *Keeping Graduate Programs Responsive to National Needs.*
New Directions for Higher Education, no. 46. San Francisco: Jossey-Bass, June 1984.

Second, they have taken advantage of new knowledge and changing perceptions in humanistic research to create new, innovative fields of study within the traditional disciplines.

Third, they have responded to new demands in the job market by creating new options or by modifying old programs.

Fourth, they have embarked on what might be termed an "awareness program," designed to educate both students and nonacademic employers about the value (and usefulness) of a graduate education tion in the humanities.

Strength Through Diversity

In carrying out this strategy, the humanities have been able to draw on two fundamental sources of strength. The first is the commitment of people in the disciplines, and of people like Yale University President A. Barlett Giamatti (1979), to the essential value of the humanities to civilization. The second is the incredible diversity of humanities graduate programs.

Several hundred colleges and universities offer graduate work in the humanities, ranging from small, off-campus Master of Liberal Arts programs to large, research-intensive Ph.D. programs. The thousands of different graduate programs allow for a great deal of experimentation in reacting to society's demands and in creating programs that will advance knowledge in emerging humanities-based disciplines.

Naturally, some of the experiments have not been successful. Some have fulfilled an immediate need and then been phased out. Others were based on a misapprehension of a social need, a miscalculation of the job market, or simply bad judgment of the value of a scholarly field of inquiry. But the diversity of institutions and offerings has helped the graduate enterprise in the humanities to transcend isolated failures.

New Program Developments

New knowledge has always caused the development of new fields of study in the humanities. The recognition that women's contribution to the humanities has been inadequately treated resulted in the development of several women's studies programs in the last decade. Various area studies programs — American studies, Latin American studies, Victorian studies, and so forth — were developed for the same reason. Recognition of the value of periodicals study in literary criticism, history, sociology, and allied areas stimulated the establishment of periodicals research as a respected interdisciplinary field of study. These and other new programs have been integrated into traditional graduate disciplines; students generally enter into them to prepare themselves for a lifetime career of research and teaching.

New programs to meet emerging social needs are not intended to replace these studies; rather, they are intended to supplement them and to extend them into new areas. The innovative programs described in the following discussion represent some of the ways in which the humanities are responding to changes in society's and students' needs. In some cases, these adaptations consist of the development of new, applied humanities-based programs—the third response in the strategy presented at the beginning of this chapter. In others, they consist of counseling and education programs aimed at students and employers in order to open up new areas of employment—the fourth response.

Because it would be impossible to describe new programs in all of the many disciplines that make up the humanities, the following discussion covers program developments in four disciplines that have traditionally been considered at the heart of humanistic study: music, philosophy, history, and literature. The discussion here is by no means comprehensive. The programs described represent what is taking place at just a few of the hundreds of colleges and universities engaged in humanities graduate education.

Music. Traditionally, graduate students in music are educated to be better teachers or better performers. But many university faculty members in music are recommending courses in the business of music both as a necessary part of a student's graduate education and as a helpful wedge for music students to use in getting jobs in business or industry. In fact, Yale, American University, Michigan, Indiana, and seven other institutions offer master's degrees—generally Master of Arts Administration degrees—with a music emphasis. The State University of New York—Binghamton offers a master of fine arts with an arts administration (including music) emphasis.

Programs in the business of music include courses in such diverse areas as marketing, music merchandising, management and administration, record production, physics of sound, legal considerations (copyrights, union contracts, and so on), film scoring, performing arts management, and many more. Most programs require internships. Business of music programs are obvious examples of interdisciplinary cooperation—among management, music, law, and other faculties—to create a field of study that American society has found to be useful. At the same time, it has taken advantage of the musical expertise and education of a significant number of graduate students. Besides the eleven schools offering graduate degrees, over 160 offer courses on some aspect of the business of music.

Many music departments are encouraging students to take computer classes as part of their advanced education. Music education faculty are still studying ways in which computers may be adapted to instruction. Composition and arrangement courses have, of course, found them to be extremely useful.

Another emerging field of graduate study and research is music therapy, an interdisciplinary area combining psychology, sociology, medicine, and music. Spearheaded by research and education at Michigan State University, music therapy aims at using music as an integral part of therapy programs for the elderly, the retarded, the disabled, and others in need. Widespread development of graduate programs is hampered by the lack of opportunities for undergraduates to study in the field; however, music educators expect that music therapy programs will develop rapidly as the results of research into the effects of music therapy are made known.

The development of these new programs should not be taken to indicate that the traditional field for master's of arts and master's of music — public school teaching — is glutted. On the contrary, according to Christopher von Baeyer (1983) of the Washington State University music faculty, the job outlook for public school teaching is positive. The recent recession has caused thousands of public schools to eliminate music faculty positions. With economic recovery should come a reinstatement of positions and a demand for faculty members to fill them.

Philosophy. Philosophy's new programs, like many in the humanities, concentrate on applied study. The major new orientation in philosophy is toward ethics studies — courses and, indeed, entire degree programs concentrating on ethical choices in decision making in professions such as medicine, law, and business. The new curricula may be based in traditional philosophy departments, in professional schools, or as part of genuine interdisciplinary programs.

The philosophy department at the University of Tennessee now has a medical ethics option at both the Ph.D. and the master's levels, an option that includes some clinical or clinic-related experience at the University of Tennessee Medical School. The Department of Biomedical History at the University of Washington's School of Medicine offers work not only in the history of medicine but also in biomedical ethics and medical jurisprudence as well. The interdisciplinary Center for Ethics and Public Policy at the University of Colorado has an "associated" graduate program at both the master's and Ph.D. levels.

Perhaps the most ambitious applied philosophy program is

offered by Bowling Green State University's philosophy department. With the help of a development grant from the National Endowment for the Humanities (NEH), Bowling Green has established a special master's program that includes the following components:

- A two-semester applied philosophy sequence incorporating treatment of applied philosophy issues, the teaching of philosophy, and the relationship between philosophy and non-academic employment
- An internship in the individual student's area of interest
- A thesis that addresses philosophically one of the problems or issues that arises during the internship.

The strongest of the applied philosophy programs are those that integrate the technical expertise of the particular profession with a strong philosophy education. Part of the technical expertise education should be taught in an internship, the traditional capstone to applied education. It is too soon to judge the effectiveness of such programs; however, as society comes more and more to the realization that business, industry, government, and the professions have a social responsibility and that decision makers in all professions need a background in making socially responsible choices, these programs could well become extremely important.

History. Like their philosopher cousins, historians have begun altering traditional history department programs to include concentration in applied history. History departments have also begun to develop better counseling programs for graduate students, programs designed to prepare students to seek nonacademic employment after graduation.

The public-history graduate track at Washington State University (WSU) is a model applied history program. The WSU history department defines public history as work in historical resources management and applied research. This historical resources management field involves the collection, preservation, and use of materials from the past by historians working in archives, museums, historical societies, and parks, in preservation planning, research, and publication. In applied research, historians undertake contract research and writing for clients who realize the need to apply the historian's perspective to problem solving, policy analysis, and project and institutional biographies.

The graduate program in public history requires that students enroll in core courses in public-history theory and methodology and in a seminar. Course work in architecture, urban planning, historical archeology, law, policy analysis, cultural resource management, and others may be taken in related departments. Students in both the master's and the Ph.D. programs are required to serve at least a one-semester internship with an appropriate agency, business, or organization.

Many history departments, acutely aware of the difficulty in placing students in faculty positions, begin counseling students at the time of their admission to graduate status to prepare themselves for non-academic employment. Such preparation may taken the form of adding marketing, guidance and counseling, business management and other similar courses to their history core, not as an integral part of the degree program but as supplemental training, as it were. Preparation may also be simply in the form of altered expectations: Graduate students are prepared to apply for a variety of nonacademic jobs and to receive help either from the department or the placement center in writing appropriate letters and compiling resumés.

Literature. An informal 1983 survey of selected English departments revealed that little new formal academic programming is being done in traditional graduate preparation in literature. Master's programs in composition and in Teaching English as a Second Language (TESL) have been developed, of course, and some institutions have worked out Ph.D. programs with a concentration in the teaching of writing. But English departments have always had the responsibility of preparing composition and language teachers. Most of these programs at the graduate level are merely a formalization of a longstanding academic practice. In curriculum modification, some departments are now offering training in computer programming and operation, either as a component of the research methods course or as a separate course taught in cooperation with the computer science department. But no major initiative toward "applied literature" (in the sense of applied philosophy or history) seems to be developing.

Instead, most English departments are reacting to the academic employment squeeze either by reducing their enrollments through more selective admissions (an admirable, if passive, response) or by instituting intensive counseling programs and workshops designed, like those in history, to prepare graduate students to seek nonacademic employment.

One of the leaders in developing counseling and workshop programs was the English department at the University of Kansas. For several years, G. D. Atkins directed a series of two sets of alternative career workshops for humanities graduate students: One consisted of talks by former graduate students in the humanities who were successfully employed outside of teaching; the other consisted of talks by executives and personnel officials who outlined what they required in potential employees and helped humanities graduate students assess opportunities in the nonacademic job market.

In 1981 the university received an NEH grant to conduct an expanded set of workshops for the Mid-America State Universities Association (MASUA, consisting of Iowa State, Kansas, Kansas State, Missouri, Nebraska, Oklahoma, and Oklahoma State). The MASUA conference, held for the benefit of graduate directors, department heads, and placement people as well as graduate students, included nationally recognized experts on alternative careers for humanists — people like Lewis Solmon, Dexter Whitehead, C. W. Kersey, Jr., Mary Hayes Somers, and Ward Hellstrom. A second conference, designed to assess the effect of the first one on each campus and to plot a further course, was held in November 1983.

The University of Kansas now employs a full-time assistant director in the placement center whose primary responsibility is to advise graduate students in the humanities. In addition, the College of Liberal Arts and Sciences has established a humanities placement committee. Both of these innovations have been effective in helping humanities graduates cope with the depressed job market.

A Final Note on New Developments

By their nature, the humanities deal with subjects that are not readily applicable to practical problems. Humanities research does not lead to "useful" conclusions in the applied sense. Consequently, applied humanities programs will always be limited in scope; public history and applied philosophy will not be the mainline options in most graduate education and research in those fields any more than computer programming will be in mathematics departments. This is not to say that the new applied program developments in the humanities are not sound or valuable; it is only to say that they are no panacea for the employment squeeze for humanities postgraduates.

In the long run, the counseling sessions for students and the aggressive efforts by Solmon, Kersey, and others to inform the non-academic community of the value of and the values in humanities graduate education may be the best of the new developments. Some far-sighted employers like William Cook, vice-president for management information systems at Morgan Stanley and Company, and Samuel Solomon, vice-president at Lehman Brothers, Kuehn and Loeb have made a company policy of hiring people with humanities graduate degrees and training them. As the counseling programs reveal a challenging, satisfying work place outside of academics to humanities graduate students, the programs may well succeed in supplying people like Cook and Solomon with the very best humanities graduates.

References

Fulton, R. D. Unpublished survey, 1983.
Giamatti, A. B. "On Behalf of the Humanities." *Profession 79,* 1979, 14–16.
von Baeyer, C. Personal communication, 1983.

Richard D. Fulton is assistant dean of the graduate school at Washington State University. In 1982–83, he served as dean in residence for the Council of Graduate Schools in the United States.

The power and authority of the graduate school can profoundly affect the quality of graduate programs in schools of education and the freedom to innovate them.

Graduate Programs in Schools of Education: Facing Tomorrow, Today

Barbara L. Schneider

Colleges and universities are now entering the most challenging and difficult times as they are forced to respond to declines in graduate school enrollments, scarcity of externally funded fellowships, and reductions in outside research support. These problems are particularly acute for graduate programs in the social sciences and perhaps most onerous for graduate programs in schools or colleges of education. In addition to these conditions, the decline of enrollments in teacher preparation programs and the national criticism directed toward the quality of these programs have had reverberating financing consequences for graduate programs in schools of education. Substantial cuts in the operating budgets of most schools of education have become a yearly reality, the difference being one of degree. These financial pressures are having a strong impact on graduate requirements and programmatic offerings in many schools of education.

During the past few years, several researchers have been conducting a national study on the "Quality of the Doctorate in Schools of Education" (Schneider and others, 1983; Ball and others, 1982). This

M. J. Pelczar, L. C. Solmon (Eds.). *Keeping Graduate Programs Responsive to National Needs.*
New Directions for Higher Education, no. 46. San Francisco: Jossey-Bass, June 1984.

study, initiated by school of education deans representing thirty-seven major research universities, focuses on determining what characterizes quality doctoral programs in the field of education. To obtain this information, the researchers have used a series of questionnaires, interviews, and on-site visits with administrators, faculty, students, and alumni. Through this study, the ways in which graduate programs in schools of education within research universities are responding to demographic and financial pressures have become evident.

The study has revealed that graduate programs in schools of education are shaped in part by the institutional size, affiliation, location, and, most important, by the mission and status of the university in which the school of education is located (Schneider, 1983). Since no two institutions share all of these characteristics, it is not surprising that, while all the graduate programs require qualifying exams and defensible dissertations, the processes by which these are accomplished are quite diverse. Even though the graduate programs operate differently, in all instances the opportunities for change seem to be constrained by two conditions: (1) the power and authority of the graduate school and (2) the qualifications and interests of students seeking graduate degrees in education. These two conditions greatly influence how schools of education can respond to financial and demographic pressures.

The Power of the Graduate School

Although graduate programs in schools of education share the problems of other graduate programs, they can and do respond to these pressures quite differently than do their academic counterparts. To a certain extent, this is the result of their function as graduate professional schools that train and credential educational practitioners — for example, school superintendents, business managers, and school counselors, among others. This training mission often affords many schools of education considerable programmatic and procedural autonomy. However, for schools of education within research universities, this presents problems as well as opportunities.

Unlike many other professional schools (such as medicine or law) located in research universities, most schools of education are controlled to some extent by the graduate schools within their institutions. Graduate student admission policies, programmatic requirements, and offerings within the school of education are often executed under the auspices of the graduate school. As a consequence, schools of education are expected to, and often do, operate similarly to the social, physical, and biological science units on campus with respect to their graduate programs.

The authority and power of the graduate school may have a profound effect on the control schools of education have over their graduate policies. For example, in each institution in our sample of thirty-seven schools of education, the graduate school was responsible for monitoring all Ph.D. degree programs. In seventeen of the twenty-seven schools where the Ph.D. and the doctor of education (Ed.D.) degrees were offered, the graduate school monitored both Ph.D. and Ed.D. programs. In only ten cases did the school of education exclusively control the Ed.D. programs.

The extent of the monitoring powers of the graduate school varied across institutions (Brown, 1983). For example, graduate schools approve doctoral committees, name committee chairs, appoint graduate school representatives with voting powers to these committees, and initiate and conduct reviews of degree programs. Some graduate schools are so influential that they control or prevent the development of new programs in schools of education. Others are viewed as nettlesome bureaucracies requiring the submission of numerous forms and other letters.

If the graduate school has a great deal of power over doctoral study and in fact wields that power, the effect in changes on school policies can be considerable. The graduate school can constrain efforts by the school of education to raise or lower admission standards, offer evening or weekend courses for graduate credit, lengthen or shorten residency requirements, or initiate or terminate program areas of specialization. These actions can be a disincentive for attracting and maintaining graduate students, which ultimately can reduce the school's financial base.

For example, in several institutions, the graduate school strictly enforces full-time residency requirements for the Ph.D. degree among all units on campus. This limits recruitment strategies for schools of education trying to attract quality practitioners from various applied areas. Practitioners are often unwilling to fulfill full-time residency requirements because of financial pressures or are unable to because their place of employment does not grant leaves of absence.

The power of graduate schools may also extend in some institutions to master's level programs. This is particularly troublesome for some schools of education, caught between the demands of state certification programs and the regulations of their graduate schools, who might not share the state's criteria for what constitutes a graduate experience. This is particularly the case for internships, observations, or off-campus experiences often required by the state authorities.

Schools of education vary in their perceptions about the value of a powerful graduate school. At some institutions, the graduate school is viewed as the legitimate mediator for in-school controversies over establishing new graduate requirements or programs. Often the graduate school policies are viewed as the standard by which the school of education must be held accountable. In contrast, other schools of education perceive the powers of the graduate school as coercive, unfair, and inappropriate for a professional school.

The point is that the graduate school represents a major or primary constraint on what a school of education can do. No matter how pressured schools of education are to raise admission standards or to initiate preparation programs for science or math educators, these goals will have to be accomplished in cooperation with graduate schools. This may or may not strengthen the quality of graduate education programs in schools of education.

The Effect of the Market

New Populations. A second major constraint on schools of education has been the marketplace. Credit hour-driven budgets, which depend on large student enrollments, have forced many schools of education to accommodate the demands of the marketplace. Schools of education have increasingly found that they must be responsive to changes in the graduate school population. Changes in the demographic, racial, and ethnic characteristics of the graduate student population in schools of education are partially reflective of population changes in American society. The application pool of potential graduate students continues to become increasingly older and more representative of women, minorities, and foreign students.

Students today are seeking graduate degrees in education for a variety of reasons. Some students are mainly in master's programs because they need a graduate degree for job security and other fringe benefits. For example, in several states, school districts require that all beginning teachers with a bachelor's degree complete a master's degree within a six-year period in order to remain in the school system. Generally, the majority of students seeking the Ph.D. or Ed.D. degree are interested in obtaining a credential for career advancement. However, the credential is being sought increasingly by individuals not in traditional education fields.

For example, among the applicant pool of many schools of education are increasing numbers of nurses and other health professionals. The American Nursing Association strongly advocates that nurse educators obtain a Ph.D. degree. In the United States there are only a relatively small number of nursing schools that offer a doctorate degree in nursing. These programs tend to prepare graduates as nursing researchers rather than as clinicians or administrators. There are also a few programs that offer a doctorate of nursing science. These programs tend to be clinically oriented and do not have the status of a Ph.D. in nursing or some other discipline. Because the advanced degree in nursing is limited to pure research, clinic work, or, in a very few instances, nursing education administration, nurse educators interested in administration, evaluation, or curriculum have matriculated to graduate programs in education.

The number of other health professionals who manage education programs in hospitals, halfway houses, and institutional care facilities is also increasing. These individuals usually matriculate in administration programs. Many schools of education have attracted a growing number of individuals from business and industry, such as those who work in personnel and continuing education departments in banks or corporations.

Traditional departments such as school administration and curriculum studies continue to attract a number of students interested in advancing in their careers as school practitioners. Some of these departments, however, have lost school business managers who prefer a master's in business administration (M.B.A.) to a Ph.D. degree. Many school districts have also caught the M.B.A. fever, and they strongly encourage their financial planners and middle managers to obtain a master's in business administration.

In areas such as school psychology, the number of students applying for a Ph.D. is increasing. Applicants to these programs, particularly in those counseling programs that have American Psychological Association approval, are not necessarily interested in pursuing careers as school counselors. Many individuals in these programs are interested in obtaining the Ph.D. so that they can establish or affiliate themselves with private psychological counseling services.

While pursuing the Ph.D. degree for many different reasons and choosing diverse programs to accomplish their objectives, students share several common characteristics. In contrast to media and commission reports, applicants to graduate programs in many schools of education have high Graduate Record Examinations scores and excellent undergraduate records. At one institution, the dean of the graduate school remarked that the Ph.D. students in education are among the best of all Ph.D. students on the campus.

While the quality of the students remains high, the opportunities for institutional or outside research support for graduate students in schools of education are limited. The small number of assistantships and fellowships has continued to decline. Consequently, many students can only attend graduate schools on a part-time basis. As a result, many schools of education have altered their restrictions on part-time course work. Evening and special weekend classes are now commonplace even in the most conservative institutions.

In addition to part-time class work, many schools of education have also relaxed their residency requirements or the policing of them. Some schools of education, which at one time required a minimum two-year full-time residency requirement for all Ph.D. students, now permit modified programs. In these programs, Ph.D. students are considered to be fulfilling the full-time requirement even though they continue to work at their place of employment and take a reduced course load. In some schools, the rules for full-time residency have remained unchanged; however, only a fraction of the students comply with the regulations, and those that do not rarely suffer any repercussions.

While these now populations are growing, the number of students seeking positions as professors has declined in some institutions and stabilized in others. This is probably not too unfortunate, as the number of faculty positions has remained relatively small in most areas. No matter what the career aspirations of the applicant are, whether professional or research-oriented, the overwhelming majority of doctoral students prefer Ph.D. to Ed.D. degrees. In institutions where the Ed.D. and Ph.D. are offered, the majority of deans reported that there were no substantive differences between the two degrees (Hood and Denny, 1983). If the number of practitioners in Ph.D. programs who are interested in pursuing professional rather than research careers continues to grow and the number in Ed.D. programs continues to decline, the integrity of the Ph.D. as a research degree will be highly suspect, regardless of programmatic offerings and requirements. In the future, it may become nearly impossible on the basis of degree to distinguish between those who are trained and planning to pursue research activities and those who are literate consumers of research and interested in working in applied areas of education.

New Programs. As the population of schools of education has changed, so have the programs. In response to new populations, some schools have created programs in allied health fields, nursing education, and human resource training. Not all schools respond only to market demands; some have begun creating programs for future societal needs and issues of national concern. In many schools, new programs and in-service workshops centering on computer technology (for example, computer literacy, programming, and teaching) are being developed in consort with state education departments and faculty from other disciplinary units outside of education.

According to several national reports, the lack of qualified science and math teachers in secondary schools is approaching crisis proportions. Several schools of education are actively responding to this situation by establishing new relations with the math, physical science, and biological science departments, designing new programs for secondary teacher training, and creating new strategies for recruiting engineers, mathematicians, and scientists into teacher preparation programs.

These examples indicate that schools of education are trying to withstand demographic and financial pressures that have the potential of seriously undermining the quality of educational experiences at both graduate and undergraduate levels. In response to these pressures, schools of education are creating programs in nontraditional areas, establishing relationships with other departments, and recruiting and supporting students outside of school-related areas. How successful schools of education will be is predicated not only on their efforts but also on how resistant graduate schools are to their plans and how responsive the market is to their initiatives.

References

Ball, C., Brown, L., Denny, T., Hood, S., Mathis, B. C., Schmidt, W., and Schneider, B. L. "The Nature and Quality of Doctoral Study in Education." Paper presented at the annual meeting of the American Educational Research Association, New York, 1982.

Brown, L. "Doctoral Study in Research-Oriented Schools of Education: The Role of the Dean." Paper presented at the annual meeting of the American Association of Colleges for Teacher Education, Detroit, February 1983.

Hood, S., and Denny, T. "The Goals of Doctoral Programs Held by Deans of Schools of Education." Paper presented at the annual meeting of the American Association of Colleges for Teacher Education, Detroit, February 1983.

Schneider, B. L. "Schools of Education: Establishing a Legitimate and Appropriate Position in the University Structure." Paper presented at the annual meeting of the American Association of Colleges for Teacher Education, Detroit, February 1983.

Schneider, B. L., Brown, L., Denny, T., Mathis, B. C., and Schmidt, W. "The Dean's Perspective: Challenges to Perceptions of Status of Schools of Education." *Phi Delta Kappa,* in press.

Barbara L. Schneider is an assistant professor of administration and policy studies in the School of Education at Northwestern University. She currently is the chair of the study of the "Quality of the Doctorate in Schools of Education."

Engineering education is going through a difficult period
because of burgeoning undergraduate enrollments, falloff in
nonforeign graduate students, and rapidly changing technology.

Graduate Education in Engineering

George E. Dieter

Starting in the mid 1970s and continuing through the recession of the early 1980s employment opportunities for Bachelor of Science (B.S.) graduates in engineering have been numerous at a time when jobs in most other fields have been decreasing relative to the overall supply of B.S. graduates. As a result, undergraduate engineering enrollments have burgeoned. From 1972 to 1982 full-time undergraduates in engineering increased from 195,000 to 403,000. Many institutions have placed limitations on undergraduate enrollment in order to preserve quality, but it is clear that the engineering education system has been severely stressed.

During the same time period, full-time graduate enrollment has increased from 36,000 to 50,000. The very strong job market at the B.S. level has attracted many of the best young graduates into industry and away from graduate school. Their places have been taken by foreign nationals. In the fall of 1982, full-time foreign nationals accounted for 32 percent of the master's enrollment and 41 percent at the Ph.D. level. Fifty percent of the doctorates in engineering in 1981–82 were awarded to foreign nationals and 18 percent of engineering faculty members received their B.S. degrees outside of the United States (Geils, 1983).

M. J. Pelczar, L. C. Solmon (Eds.). *Keeping Graduate Programs Responsive to National Needs.*
New Directions for Higher Education, no. 46. San Francisco: Jossey-Bass, June 1984.

Delivery Systems for Graduate Programs

The pervasive growth of the computer industry and the rapid development of such high-technology fields as biotechnology, communications, composite materials, microelectronics, and robotics have placed a premium on access to graduate engineering programs. In such high-technology areas, continual training and renewal of the engineering staff is vital. Thus, although many of the brightest B.S. graduates are forsaking full-time graduate studies, there is a growing demand for quality part-time programs. Several delivery systems have been developed in response to this need for providing off-campus access to graduate courses.

Instructional television (ITV) is the most common delivery system. It was pioneered at the University of Florida in 1964, and currently over fourteen universities deliver live graduate courses over microwave channels (usually in the ITFS frequency band of 2.5 gigahertz) to off-campus locations (Down, 1976). Off-campus locations typically are provided with telephone talk-back to ask questions in real time. Between 1970 and 1980 over 2,800 master's degrees in engineering were awarded in off-campus programs using ITV (Baldwin and Down, 1981). The effectiveness of ITV as a delivery system has been studied by Schramm (1972).

Videotape instruction at off-campus locations is another common delivery system. Tapes are prepared in on-campus classrooms with live classes and are delivered to the off-campus locations by courier or mail. With this delivery mode, the generation of the instruciton occurs at a different time than the delivery of the instruction. This flexibility in the time of receipt of instruction often is important to part-time graduate students employed in industry, but the feedback provided by telephone talk-back is lost.

To compensate for this loss of reinforcement, companies may choose to use *tutored videotape instruction* (TVI). The tutors, who view the tape with the students, are engineers on the staff of the industrial firm employing the students. While not necessarily experts in the subject of the course, they are more mature in the subject than the students. Gibbons and others (1977) present data to show that part-time students in industry using TVI can significantly outperform campus students with comparable academic records in the same course.

Plans are well underway for the establishment of a National Technological University (NTU) that will coordinate courses offered by about ten member universities and award master's degrees in various engineering disciplines (Hickerson, 1983). Courses will be offered initially by videotape instruction, but by the fall of 1985 it is expected that courses will be delivered from the sponsoring institutions to off-campus sites anywhere in the United States by television using satellite communications. This plan involves two pioneering features. It will be the first widespread use of satellite communications for the delivery of graduate courses. Also, it will combine courses produced by a number of universities into a coherent curriculum. The National Technological University will develop the curricula and advise the students through contact with faculty in member institutions, but it will conduct no classes of its own. Hopefully, it will provide instruction that is a composite of the best offered in the nation and will use modern technology to deliver it to engineers employed in locations remote from major engineering schools.

New Programs

While the basic disciplines of engineering are old and well established, there is a continual process of adaptation in engineering education as technology moves in new directions. Several major thrusts have been evident in the past five years.

The *computer area* of specialization within electrical engineering has grown in importance. Many institutions are developing programs in computer engineering that are separate from electrical engineering and computer science.

The renewed national concern with economic development, especially in light of foreign competition, has stimulated new interest in the area of *manufacturing*. Another important reason for this rejuvenation of manufacturing as a respectable engineering discipline is the major impact that the computer is having on the field. Computer-controlled machine tools and robots, as well as entire manufacturing systems controlled by computer, represent exciting areas for research by engineering faculty and students. Recently International Business Machines (IBM) has awarded ten million dollars split among five universities to develop graduate programs in manufacturing systems engineering. While it is still too early to tell how the field will develop within engineering schools, it is more likely that manufacturing engineering will evolve as an interdisciplinary program among departments like mechanical, electrical, and industrial engineering than as the establishment of new manufacturing departments.

Engineering management has been an area of very rapid growth. Since 1975 the number of master's programs in the field has increased from twenty to about 100. Engineering management programs have been developed in recognition of the fact that, for many engineers, the normal career progression takes them into management (Kocaoglu, 1980). An engineering management program differs from industrial engineering, to which it is most closely related among the engineering disciplines, by its greater focus on "people problems" rather than on "system design." It differs from the master's in business administration (M.B.A.) and other general management degrees in requiring a component of engineering-oriented courses and in having a strong mathematical and computer orientation. Most engineering management courses are designed for the part-time employed student. Indeed, many engineering management programs require lower-level management exposure for entry into the program.

Professional Education in Engineering

The structure and practice of graduate education in engineering today is much closer to that found in physics or chemistry than that found in the professions of law and medicine. Most engineering departments offer a Master of Science degree and the Ph.D. degree. Usually the degrees are administered by the graduate dean of the campus. Emphasis is on basic research and on advancing the frontier of the engineering sciences.

However, with the rapid advance of technology, there is an increasing need for better-educated engineers. It is clear that four years of undergraduate education can only provide the fundamentals upon which to build a career. Specialized subject matter, professional aspects such as ethics and communication, and design specialization must be provided for, either in subsequent formal education, in the work place, or by self-study. There has been a movement during the past ten years to establish professional schools of engineering on the basis that existing graduate education is too much oriented toward research and does not satisfy the needs of industry. Five critical requirements were proposed to distinguish such a school (Grinter, 1975). First, students should choose this path into the engineering profession knowing that the central objective is training in high-level design for a professional career. The second is that the faculty must be both up to date and fully experienced in design practice. Third, the undergraduate program should provide strong support to advance design. Fourth, the curriculum should contain at least a year of internship or practice. Fifth, the internship should precede two years of advanced study in design.

Many institutions have established Master of Engineering programs. A number of these programs were established in response to the decision of the Engineers Council for Professional Development (now the Accreditation Board for Engineering and Technology or ABET) to accredit programs at the advanced (master's) level. ABET is now phasing out advanced-level accreditation. While many of these programs have more of a design orientation than the conventional master's degree, there is no general definition of what constitutes a professional master's in engineering. Many of these programs, for example, are only one year in duration, a few require two years, some may require an internship. Moreover, there is not complete agreement as to the name of the degree. Some very professionally oriented programs are given under the usual master's designation.

About a dozen institutions offer the Doctor of Engineering (D.Engr.) degree. While there is not complete agreement, most of these programs meet the criteria described by Grinter. They require at least two years of graduate-level work and an internship. Invariably, the D.Engr. dissertation differs from that of the Ph.D. in that it is oriented more toward applications or design, rather than directed toward the development of basic knowledge. Several D.Engr. programs recommend a strong minor in management, and they view their program as a professional education for top technical managers.

The acceptance of professional engineering programs, either at the master's or doctorate level, has been modest. There is no groundswell of support for these programs on engineering faculties. Furthermore, there has not been an easy mechanism for funding these programs since they do not link well to conventional sources of university research support. Finally, the financial reward to graduates of these programs has not been sufficiently great compared with conventional engineering graduate programs to encourage students to provide their own financial support. An engineering analogue to the M.B.A degree, where students borrow and defer income in anticipation of outstanding starting salaries, has not yet arisen.

However, it could well be that the growing high-technology environment will encourage the development of professional programs in engineering. There is a renewed spirit of cooperation and partnership between industry and engineering schools. There is recognition that new technology needs to be moved quickly into the marketplace to create jobs and wealth. Engineers seem best equipped to do this, but they need other dimensions added to their education to optimize the process. Two new institutions aimed at this goal have arisen recently in the Boston area: the Wang Institute for Computer Science and the new Graduate School of Engineering Leadership. If these are successful, it could encourage established institutions to move more strongly in the direction of graduate professional education.

70

References

Baldwin, L. V., and Down, K. S. *Educational Technology in Engineering.* Washington, D.C.: National Academy Press, 1981.

Down, K. S. "The Stanford Instructional TV Network." *Engineering Education,* April 1976, pp. 762–763.

Geils, J. W. "The Faculty Shortage: 1982 Survey." *Engineering Education,* October 1983, pp. 47–53.

Gibbons, J. F., Kincheloe, W. R., and Down, K. S. "Tutored Videotape Instruction." *Science,* 1977, *195,* 1139–1146.

Grinter, L. E. "Defining a Professional School of Engineering." *Engineering Education,* January 1975, pp. 279, 354–355.

Hickerson, K. W. "New Engineering School Will Take Classroom to the Students Via Satellite." *Engineering Times,* November 1983, p. 12.

Kocaoglu, D. C. "Master's Degree Programs in Engineering Management." *Engineering Education,* January 1980, pp. 350–352.

Schramm, W. (Ed.). *Quality in Instructional Television.* Honolulu: University Press of Hawaii, 1972.

George E. Dieter is dean of the College of Engineering at the University of Maryland.

Where there are faculty shortages, audio-teleconferencing can be used effectively to bring needed knowledge to college and university classes.

A University-Industry Association Model for Curriculum Enhancement

Moses Passer

No college or university, even the most distinguished, can have outstanding strength in every facet of every subject. This is particularly true in the more rapidly advancing areas of science and engineering, where leaders in the field can be found in only a few academic institutions — or, as often as not, they are not to be found in academic settings at all. At the same time, every school wants its students to receive the best, most up-to-date education that its capabilities permit it to provide. Any mechanism that can enlarge these capabilities, without requiring more faculty or incurring other significant additional costs, should be a welcome boon to the academic process. This chapter describes how audio-teleconferencing can enlarge the capabilities of academic institutions substantially without requiring faculty growth or significant budget increases.

The author happens to be a chemist, so the illustrative examples are taken from that discipline. The observations and conclusions should apply, at least to some degree, in most other disciplines.

M. J. Pelczar, L. C. Solmon (Eds.). *Keeping Graduate Programs Responsive to National Needs.*
New Directions for Higher Education, no. 46. San Francisco: Jossey-Bass, June 1984.

Subject Matter

The following are two examples of chemistry topics that most academic institutions would probably like to make available to their students but for which only a limited number have the academic resources.

The first example is polymer science. About 70 percent of all chemistry graduates are employed in industry, and about one-half of all chemists in industry work on some aspect of polymer science. While most employers do not have any major complaints about the technical contents of their employees' education — the serious problems are in communication skills — one technical area in which they do identify a deficiency is in polymer science. It turns out, however, that only a few universities, and virtually no colleges, have any strength in this subject area; a major portion of the basic research and most of the technological advances in polymer science have been achieved in industrial laboratories. The result has been that few chemistry graduates at any level — B.A., M.S., or Ph.D. — complete their formal education with much background in one of the most important areas of modern chemical science and technology.

Modern information science represents a second major void in the academic preparation of chemists. The gathering, storage, and retrieval of information are undergoing revolutionary changes, and many of the major innovations are taking place outside of academic circles. In chemistry, for example, the most fundamental and far-reaching developments in information science are probably occurring at the Chemical Abstracts Service of the American Chemical Society. It is quite clear that all students — not only in chemistry, not only in the science and engineering disciplines in general, but everywhere on campus — need instruction in modern information science as part of their college curriculum. It is equally clear that few universities have the capability to provide this instruction.

Comparable voids can be identified elsewhere in chemistry education, and equally significant voids are likely to exist in many other disciplines.

The Proposal

The American Chemical Society (ACS) proposes to attack the problem by (1) developing ACS Audio — Teleconference Courses in the needed subjects and (2) delivering these courses nationwide to colleges and universities.

ACS Audio-Teleconference Courses. ACS operates a large and varied array of continuing education programs. These include three mature programs — Short Courses, Audio Courses, and Video Courses — and two programs in the early development stage — Computer Courses and Audio-Teleconference Courses (or ATC Courses). Three of the programs — Audio, Video, and Computer — use electronic technologies in which the teachers are not present in real time. In the other two programs — Short Courses and ATC Courses — the teachers are available in real time, in the Short Courses by being present in the same room and in the ATC Courses through real-time access by telephone and loudspeaker. These programs are all self-sustaining; their annual budget is around $2 million; and they are administered by a staff of twelve persons.

An audio-teleconference is an expanded version of the conventional conference call; the participants at each site are groups equipped with audio amplifiers instead of individuals with telephones. The continuous audio access of each site with all the others is the same in both types of conference call. (A video-teleconference is similar, but it has the added dimension of visual communication, usually one-way.) As a specific example, ACS recently presented an ATC course in which thirteen cities were linked together. A team of four teachers presented the course, each from a different city. The course was delivered to groups of practicing chemists in nine cities; one of the nine groups was assembled by a university, and the rest were employee groups on the premises of their employers.

Three ATC courses had been completed as of November 1983, and the results have been most encouraging in two major respects: (1) This delivery mode appears to be highly effective pedagogically, and (2) the prospects are very favorable that the program will soon become financially self-sustaining, at least when delivery is to industry clients.

Advantages. ATC courses offer the following advantages over alternate delivery systems for academic subject matter:

1. Teacher availability — The outstanding authorities for aspects of any given subject can be recruited as the teaching team for that subject — no matter what their affiliation or where they might be located. They can be in academia (and not necessarily all at the same institution), in industry, in government, or elsewhere. Recruitment is made easier by the fact that the time demand on each individual teacher is minimal, since he or she lectures from the office or from home — no travel is necessary.
2. Modest costs — Since neither the teachers nor the students

have to travel out of town, the major cost component of a short course is completely eliminated. The substitute cost for equipment and for long-distance telephone is much lower than these travel costs. This cost advantage has already enabled ACS to bring ATC courses to small communities where it had never before been feasible to bring in-person short courses.

3. Intermittent scheduling — Unlike in-person short courses, which must be scheduled for concentrated periods of several consecutive full days, ATC courses can be scheduled on the usual academic pattern — say, one hour per day three times a week for several weeks.

Disadvantages. ATC courses are not a panacea — they do have certain weaknesses:

1. Absence of teacher — No electronic device, no matter how good, can substitute for a teacher who is present in person.
2. Acceptability — Some participants, at least initially, find the technology threatening. In most cases, however, the resistance wears off quite rapidly.

Audio Versus Video. Video-teleconferencing bears the same relationship, approximately, to audio-teleconferencing as television bears to radio. On the other hand, transmission rates for video are much higher than for audio — so much higher as to be prohibitive for the relatively small populations that comprise the ACS clientele.

It turns out, however, that most of the audio-video accessibility gap can be traversed by supplying the students with first-rate supplementary visuals that are sent out to each group in advance. These usually consist of slides, which are shown during the session, or printed backup materials that contain all the visuals that the speaker intends to use.

Video transmission rates are declining rapidly, so what is prohibitive today might not be prohibitive in the near future. This does not necessarily mean that the ACS courses will immediately drop audio in favor of video, since the combination of audio and auxiliary print material seems to be working so well. The audio-video choice would be made, when and if video transmission rates decline significantly, on the basis of the evidence available at that time.

How to Provide Audio-Teleconferencing. As indicated earlier, the American Chemical Society proposes to develop ACS ATC courses in needed subjects and to deliver these courses to academic institutions. Once a network of participating colleges and universities is set up, the system has tremendous versatility, as is suggested by the following illustration.

Assume, for example, that ACS develops just two courses, A

and B. Assume further that each course can be offered at the under-graduate level (U), the graduate level (G), the continuing education level for chemists in industry and for college teachers (C), and with yet another version for high school teachers (H). All of these groups, and many more, could easily be accommodated on a single ATC network. The following is just one hypothetical schedule of the many that could be arranged.

M,W,F	9–10 A.M.	A–U
M,W,F	10–11 A.M.	B–U
T,Th	9–10 A.M.	A–G
T,Th	10–11 A.M.	B–G
M,W	4–6 P.M.	A–C
T,Th	4–6 P.M.	B–C
Sat	Mornings	A–H
Sat	Afternoons	B–H

It should be noted that there is equal versatility in the composition of the receiving network. Each participating institution has the right to receive whatever combination of sessions it finds most desirable.

Academic Control. ACS's only role is to develop and deliver the courses to the cooperating institutions. Once a course reaches the campus, each receiving institution has full control. It applies its own registration and tuition procedures; its own faculty conducts discussion and review sessions, administers examinations, and makes all decisions on grades and academic credit.

By the same token, an industry group receiving the same course at the same time would probably administer it differently. Typically, it would probably elect not to give examinations, grades, or credit.

The important point is that each receiving group has full control to administer the course exactly in the manner that best fits its own circumstances.

Why an Association

It seems quite clear that any major academic institution that happens to be strong in a particular subject could equally well transmit ATC courses to a network of receivers. What, then, is the advantage of an association such as ACS? One important advantage is that an association does not carry the N.I.H. ("not invented here") burden: Ohio

State might not want to receive a Michigan State course and vice versa, but each might be quite willing to receive a course developed and transmitted by the American Chemical Society. A second advantage is the ability of a national association to assemble a teaching team recruited from several sources, including more than one academic institution, industry, and so on.

Moses Passer is director of the Education Division of the American Chemical Society in Washington, D.C.

Now more than ever, there is a place for the well-educated individual in business and industry; the problem lies in breaking down the long-established barriers between academia and business.

Opportunities for New Careers: The Academic in the World of Business

Clinton W. Kersey

Structural changes in the economy have so altered the traditional ways of doing business that the survival of entire industries is now at stake. Those businesses that perform a legitimate economic function and perform it well are likely to survive. However, "the key to survival," as Robert Rittereiser of Merrill Lynch says, ". . . is directly tied to a firm's quality of planning, adaptability to change, and an honest appraisal of its strengths and weaknesses" (Committee to Examine the Future Structure. . . , 1982, p. 40). So amidst the outcry for an increase in American productivity and better cooperation between management and labor, one also hears of the need for bright, well-educated people who are eager to accept positions of responsibility in a variety of organizations. As one government official recently said, "Basically, we'll be pushing a well-educated and trained and retrained work force as the best industrial policy this nation can have" (Anderson and others, 1983, p. 99).

Remarks such as these should leave Ph.D.s in the arts and sciences feeling optimistic about their future; the knowledge and skills

M. J. Pelczar, L. C. Solmon (Eds.). *Keeping Graduate Programs Responsive to National Needs.*
New Directions for Higher Education, no. 46. San Francisco: Jossey-Bass, June 1984.

needed to complete one's graduate education are precisely those needed to solve the complex problems facing business and industry today. For example, quality planning involves paying attention to detail and learning to manage one's time and resources effectively. Adaptability to change requires tenacity, perseverance, and a willingness to learn throughout one's life on one's own. Similarly, an honest appraisal of an organization's strengths and weaknesses requires good analytical skills and the ability to communicate in conversation and in writing.

Ph.D.s should feel optimistic about the future for other reasons as well. Besieged by foreign competitors, companies need employees who possess cross-cultural skills and who are accustomed to stiff competition. Since many companies are re-examining the markets they serve, they also need people who understand the complexities of research and appreciate the social dimensions of problems. Moreover, they need people who can make discriminating judgments now that business finds itself in the information age. Once the flow of information is accelerated and access to it is increased, an organization's ability to make critical decisions can be substantially reduced unless there are individuals who can take a large amount of data and quickly consolidate them into a useful form.

The Stereotype of the Ivory Tower —
Barriers in Business Attitudes

Although Ph.D.s in the arts and sciences possess the knowledge and skills that business and industry need, certain attitudes and practices discourage nonacademic employers from taking advantage of them. The business community's tendency to focus on jobs rather than careers is one inhibiting factor. Companies often measure success in terms of their quarterly profits. Consequently, they place more emphasis on accomplishing short-term objectives than on achieving long-term goals. This means that a person's value to an organization is judged in terms of one's short-term benefit instead of one's long-term potential. With little or no thought given to what will become of individuals once these objectives have been met, employers hire persons because of their job-related skills rather than their ability to accept a broad range of responsibilities over time.

The desire to establish and maintain strict divisions of labor is another factor that prevents employers from utilizing the knowledge and skills of academics. When the landscape of American business was familiar and a company's problems were well defined, employers found it unnecessary to use people in creative ways, particularly those with backgrounds dissimilar to their own. Although the landscape has now changed and many business problems are less clearly defined, employers still prefer hiring individuals who fit into traditional categories and who are eager to move within an organization along well-established lines.

In addition, many employers view Ph.D.s as belonging to an elitist group that has little interest in the practical matters with which business must deal daily. The natural tendency to like persons similar to oneself reinforces this stereotype; employers thus tend to hire individuals with whom they have a great deal in common.

Finally, employers are reluctant to hire Ph.D.s because many Ph.D.s lack experience in working in groups, and some of them lack the interpersonal skills needed for success in business. Particularly in the humanities and social sciences, where emphasis is placed upon one's own research, students are not given enough opportunity to work within groups or to develop fully their interpersonal skills. Employers view this as a liability because one's success or failure in business ultimately depends upon one's ability to render personalized service and to become an integral part of a team.

Barriers in the Attitudes of Academics

On the other hand, some of the factors limiting the career options of academics can be traced directly to their own attitudes and perceptions. At a time when rapid change is creating greater opportunities for well-educated men and women, only a small percentage of those in academia are exploring their full range of options, despite the growing concern over the shortage of teaching positions in higher education.

Some academics do not explore their options because they are unaware of the revolution occurring around them and of the challenging opportunities that it creates. Unfamiliar with the language and principles of business, these persons have difficulty identifying those companies that can use their skills. The task of matching their skills to an organization's needs is made unnecessarily difficult, simply because they know very little about the organizations and the people to whom they are presenting themselves.

Further, many academics are reluctant to overcome this lack of familiarity with business because they doubt that they can locate a position consistent with their values and interests — they doubt that they can find, in the business world, issues and persons as challenging as those found in higher education or that they can secure a job that both pays well and enables them to maintain a sense of integrity. This fear reflects an assumption that business is a virtual wasteland and that greed is the sole motivator of persons employed by profit-making organizations. These misconceptions have many sources — one being the literature of the humanities and social sciences, which often presents a negative image of business, another being faculty members who insist that graduate students are wasting a valuable education unless they emulate their adviser's career.

Other academics do not explore their options because they lack self-confidence. "What could a person with a Ph.D. in Slavic linguistics possibly offer the world of business?" is a question that arises because some academics have been led to believe that graduate school merely prepares an individual to teach and to conduct research. Consequently, they have become convinced that they do not possess the knowledge and skills that business values. They have also been led to believe that their value to an organization is related to the type of degree they hold. They fail to realize that employers do not hire degrees but rather individuals who can help the corporation solve problems. After a student has received the highest degree that the educational system awards, it is ironic that he or she should conclude that the acquired skills cannot be transferred to other contexts.

In other words, some academics have not learned to think flexibly and creatively about what they have to offer an employer. Failing to understand that similar functions and tasks are performed in different contexts, these individuals do not realize that they have been "selling" ideas and "marketing" courses for years. Therefore, when they present themselves to employers, all they can think to say is, "Here I am, use me!"

There are also academics who do not consider their options because they are unfamiliar with the hiring process in most nonacademic fields. Persons in higher education secure a position by having someone sponsor them — one's graduate adviser, a colleague, or a friend. It is considered improper for one to approach employers directly and express a desire to work in their department.

On the other hand, persons in business not only encourage but expect potential employees to take an active role in the hiring process. Employers take the position that, if individuals want a job badly enough, they will demonstrate their interest by being persistent. Furthermore, employers expect candidates to present their qualifications in an attractive and persuasive manner. As the senior personnel officer of a large bank recently said:

> Academics don't realize that hiring a person is like purchasing a car. An employer is presented with one set of options and then

with another — and no two are exactly alike. Consequently, persons with the responsibility for hiring are impressed with those individuals who can explain how their backgrounds satisfies the employer's needs.

Finally, there are Ph.D.s who refuse to consider their options because they fear the rejection of colleagues, family members, and friends. Exploring one's career options can be a painful and lonely experience, especially when a person is criticized for talking openly about his or her doubts and fears. Unfortunately, this is the experience of most Ph.D.s, and particularly of those who decide to leave academia. Commenting on the emotional support she failed to receive, one woman recently said:

> My greatest difficulty with the move has been emotionally based. I particularly have problems conversing with former colleagues in my field. Most people feel that I lightly tossed out a promising career. They cannot recognize the agony that went into my decision. Old friends act betrayed — how could I waste my valuable education, talent, and skills? How could I waste their investment in me? I understand some of those feelings. I nonetheless resent the lack of emotional support which I seek and and which should be there. I hate feeling like a priest who has broken his monastic vows. Knowing that I will not see my friends again — and that we part with some resentment on both sides — presents a problem for which I was not prepared.

Four Steps Toward Eliminating the Barriers

If Ph.D.s in the arts and sciences are to take full advantage of the opportunities produced by this era of rapid change, four things need to be done. First, the stereotypes that business and higher education have of one another need to be exposed for what they are — half-truths that prevent the two groups from working together in solving the complex problems confronting our society.

Second, the vocational attitude toward graduate education needs to be challenged: Who determined that Ph.D.s could only teach and conduct research upon completing their degree? Once this common notion has been challenged, perhaps the "appropriate" use of one's graduate training will not be as restrictive as it is today. This is not to say that acquiring a Ph.D. in the arts and sciences is the best means of preparing oneself for a career in business. There is no *one* way, precisely because employers need a variety of perspectives represented in the

82

decision-making process of their organizations. And there is no *best* way because it is impossible to prescribe a means of preparing oneself for careers that do not yet exist.

Third, more thought needs to be given to the ways in which Ph.D.s are trained. Specifically, Ph.D.s need the experience of working in groups, and they need additional opportunities to develop their interpersonal skills. To eliminate the crisis of confidence from which many of them suffer, graduate schools need to give Ph.D.s not only encouragement but also a process tht enables them to assess their skills and values and then to match them to an organization's needs.

Fourth, academics need to be encouraged to talk openly and freely about their career frustrations, ambitions, and goals. Moreover, they need a supportive environment in which this can be done — one that is provided on an ongoing basis and not only during a period of financial crisis.

Will rapid change be a constructive or destructive force in American business? While it is too early to tell, one thing is certain — organizations will need at their disposal the best resources that our country provides. One such resource is the unique pool of talent that higher education now supplies. If it is used properly and expeditiously, this period of transition could well be a time of opportunity and not one of despair.

References

Anderson, H., Thomas, R., Manning, R., and Leslee, C. "Making Industrial Policy." *Newsweek,* October, 24, 1983, p. 98–99.
Committee to Examine the Future Structure of the Securities Industry. *The Financial Services Industry of Tomorrow.* Washington, D.C.: National Association of Securities Dealers, 1982.

Clinton W. Kersey is the administrative director of the University of Virginia's Career Opportunities Institute, a program designed to broaden the career options of Ph.D.s in the arts and sciences.

It is time to enhance the ability of American graduate students to contribute to international communication in their fields.

International Aspects of Graduate Education

Jules B. LaPidus

This chapter examines some aspects of international education that directly affect graduate education in the United States. Programs that are inherently international in scope, such as international studies, are not discussed here except as they relate to programs that are not. Nor will I dwell on language and literature programs per se; obviously, students of the language and literature of a country different from their own need to learn that language and study that culture. But within the enormous range of disciplines, areas of concentration, and programs that constitute graduate education, there are many others that also directly involve an international dimension.

International Studies for Research-Oriented Programs

In those programs that culminate in a thesis or dissertation, the needs of the research are dominant: Scholars must learn what they need to know in order to work on the problems that attract their interest. For example, although many graduate schools no longer require that all Ph.D. candidates demonstrate competence in foreign languages, there are certainly areas of study that still demand a knowl-

M. J. Pelczar, L. C. Solmon (Eds.). *Keeping Graduate Programs Responsive to National Needs.*
New Directions for Higher Education, no. 46. San Francisco: Jossey-Bass, June 1984.

edge of other cultures and languages in order for scholars to read the relevant literature and to understand the societal context in which events occur. Neither faculty nor students would challenge the statement that graduate students studying Soviet history, Japanese art, or French politics need to know the relevant languages and cultural backgrounds. Similarly, the economist specializing in economic development in Brazil, the sociologist studying class structure in India, or the anthropologist investigating family life in Samoa needs to know the culture and language in order to pursue the problem. An international component does not have to be imposed: It is implicit.

A variety of approaches is available to ensure that graduate students in these discipines obtain the language training and the knowledge of other countries or areas of the world necessary for their work. Some universities have established language and area studies centers, in some cases funded under Title VI of the National Defense Education Act. Usually, these centers are not degree-granting units but rather they comprise groups of faculty members, from a variety of departments, whose scholarly interests are directed toward the area involved. Thus, a Center for Latin American Studies or a Slavic and East European Center may include linguists, historians, economists, political scientists, and others. These centers perform a number of functions, all of them directed toward the promotion and coordination of studies in the world area they represent. Many of them have developed graduate certificate programs that bring together language and area studies in a coherent fashion. Some of these programs are designed to be taken concurrently with a master's or Ph.D. degree in a discipline, and, in some cases, they may be considered as minors. The development of this kind of coherent program, either through a formally designated center or by a group of interested faculty, can be extremely effective in providing the appropriate international background, at the appropriate level, for scholars requiring it.

International Studies for Practitioner Programs

Graduate programs that are not research-oriented but rather are directed toward the training of practitioners are designed to meet the current and anticipated needs of the field of practice. Most programs of this type are at the master's level and are usually clearly designated. Examples are the Master of Business Administration (M.B.A.), Master of Public Health (M.P.H.), and Master of Library Science (M.L.S.). Many of these fields are becoming increasingly international.

Some students in these programs are interested in developing a specific international perspective; conversely, students in programs that are inherently international, such as language or international studies programs, may be interested in developing a specific technical competence. To accommodate both of these interests, some universities have devised integrated degree programs or have developed procedures whereby students can obtain two master's degrees, either sequentially or, through careful planning, concurrently. Burn (1980), in commenting on this approach, suggests that:

> Increasing numbers of graduate students in international and area studies earn a master's degree in this field and then pursue a graduate degree in business or in other professional fields, including law, health, and agriculture. The international and area studies centers and programs are beginning to encourage their students in this direction. Integrated or combined graduate degrees have also been developed at a few universities [p. 138].

Examples of such programs include: the three-year program leading to "twin" master of arts degrees in Graduate Library School and the Department of South Asian Languages and Civilizations at the University of Chicago; the "articulated" degree program at UCLA leading to the master's degree in African Area Studies and the master of public health; and the Master in International Business Studies (M.I.B.S.) at the University of South Carolina. The M.I.B.S. program is unique in that it combines in a single program language study, both in this country and abroad, business courses, area studies, and a six-month internship in a foreign company (overseas for American students, in the United States for foreign students). Kuhne and Jordan (1980) offer a complete description of this program.

International Communication Among All Scholars

All of the approaches discussed so far have been primarily programmatic; they have involved course work—arranged as a minor, or a certificate program, or an additional master's program, or a single integrated program—that serves to add an international component (usually some combination of language and area studies) to graduate work in a discipline or profession.

The discussion also has centered on the needs of the research or of the practice and on how universities can respond to those needs through curricular development. Shifting the focus to the generalizable knowledge base of the discipline or profession reveals another kind of need.

At its most fundamental, the theory base in any discipline can be thought of as being culture-free. Scholars and practitioners need to be aware of and contribute to the continually evolving body of theory and commentary that defines their disciplines; they need to know what their international colleagues are thinking and writing about. One of the images that graduate educators are fond of is the "invisible college"—that worldwide collection of scholars in a given discipine who, by making the results of their studies public, communicate with each other through the medium of their scholarship. There is no question that this international community of scholars really exists, but the ability of its members to communicate across language and cultural boundaries is usually most effective when the discipine has evolved a language and, in a manner of speaking, a culture of its own. Perhaps the best examples are mathematics, physics, and chemistry, whose practitioners need little more than pencil and paper to establish instant intellectual rapport, and music and dance, whose performers respond to a universal downbeat.

In all scholarly fields, however, there is a need for direct communication. Ziman (1968) expresses this beautifully, discussing science in its broadest meaning:

> The manifest internationalism of science is not a bourgeois or communist conspiracy; nor is it merely sentimentality about the Brotherhood of Man; it is inherent in the very nature of science itself, which must always seek to encompass the largest public for the knowledge it aspires to. . . . Internationalism is a primary principle of science, demanded by the inmost law of its being. To appreciate this, one has only to visit a scientific laboratory in a politically or geographically isolated country. It is not that the library lacks the proper books, or that journals arrive a little late; it is the absence of contact with the current *informal* consensus, of conversation with genuine colleagues or visitors with wild new ideas, of a reliable assessment of the quality of one's work [p. 93].

There is an absolute need to facilitate international communication among scholars; international exchange programs are one way to meet that need.

International Exchange Programs

The purpose of most international education exchange programs is to provide an impetus, a rationale, a mechanism, and, in many cases, funding so that individuals from one country can go to another for the purpose of studying or doing research. Most people who travel to other countries as participants in these programs (as well as those who do so independently) are pursuing their own professional goals. Those goals are most often directly related to their disciplines; they may be degree-oriented (as is usually the case with foreign graduate students in the United States), nondegree-oriented (as is usually the case with American graduate students in other countries), or research-oriented (as is the case with all scholars). In any event, the result is to place individuals in contact and, in the best examples, in communication with their colleagues. For most Americans, that communication is possible because, at the graduate level and above, the common language in most disciplines has often been some variant of English.

Many American graduate students and faculty members may be unaware that they are participating in international educational exchange programs. For the majority of non-Americans, participation in an exchange program means learning English and coming to the United States. For the majority of Americans, it means staying at home, speaking English, and working with foreign students and visiting scholars. This involuntary participation can be passive, which deemphasizes the international aspects, or active, which emphasizes them. In either case, although the objective of facilitating international communication at the discipline or professional level may be achieved, host faculty and students gain little or nothing in terms of the other benefits usually associated with international exchange programs. They do not gain the benefit of "internationalization"— the increased awareness and understanding that comes with learning another language and with living and working in another country.

There is widespread concern about the state of international education in this country. Most of the discussion of internationalization in America has been focused on elementary, secondary, and undergraduate education; the issues have been expressed clearly in the report of the President's Commission on Foreign Language and International Studies (1979): "Americans' scandalous incompetence in foreign language also explains our dangerously inadequate understanding of world affairs. Our schools graduate a large majority of students whose knowledge and vision stop at the American shoreline, whose approach to international affairs is provincial, and whose heads have been filled with astonishing misinformation" (p. 7).

Role of Graduate Deans

Graduate deans can play a pivotal role in fostering the development of international aspects in graduate education. In the area of academic program development, what is needed is someone to convene the interested parties, obtain their commitment, and facilitate program development. Usually this does not require the initiation of new courses or new degree programs. Costs may be minimal. Interest among faculty and prospective students can be high. The rewards, particularly in terms of improving the international competence of many of our best students, can be great. Whether the driving force is the research problem or the professional practice, we have the capabiity to develop strong and effective programs that make academic sense.

With respect to international exchange, graduate deans can help in two major ways. First, they can serve as information sources and advocates on their campuses. For example, since 1982, graduate deans have been the institutional liaison with faculty for the Senior Scholar Fulbright program. Second, they can try to find ways in which visiting scholars and foreign graduate students can enhance the international education of their American colleagues. One possibility is to sponsor continuing seminars involving visiting scholars. Another is to encourage graduate students, foreign and domestic, to participate in discussions focused on issues affecting various parts of the world. An excellent description of activities of this kind has been provided by Christensen and Thielen (1983), and Minkel and Richards (1983) have presented a succinct and cogent overview of some of the ways in which graduate schools can foster internationalism.

Graduate education is intrinsically international. The scholars who contribute to the evolution of every discipline may live in dozens of countries and speak different languages, but they are bound together by the work they share. Graduate educators, by constantly seeking ways to improve international understanding and communication, can ensure that this "invisible college" does not become a tower of Babel.

References

Burn, B. B. *Expanding the International Dimension of Higher Education.* San Francisco: Jossey-Bass, 1980.

Christensen, G. C., and Thielen, T. B. "Cross-Cultural Activities: Maximizing the Benefits of Educational Interchange." In H. M. Jenkins and Associates (Eds.) *Educating Students from Other Nations: American Colleges and Universities in International Educational Exchange.* San Francisco: Jossey-Bass, 1983.

Kuhne, R. J., and Jordan, G. P. "Integrating International Business and Language Training." *ADFL Bulletin,* 1980, *11* (3), 27–30.

Minkel, C. W., and Richards, M. P. *The International Dimensions in Graduate Education.* Chattanooga: University of Tennessee, 1983.

President's Commission on Foreign Language and International Studies. *Strength Through Wisdom: A Critique of U.S. Capability.* Washington, D.C.: Government Printing Office, 1979.

Ziman, J. M. *Public Knowledge.* Cambridge, England: Cambridge University Press, 1968.

Jules B. LaPidus is dean of the graduate school of Ohio State University.

not worth it

The functions of graduate and continuing education increasingly overlap.

Graduate Education and Continuing Education

Kenneth E. Young

The title "dean of graduate and continuing education" can be found in a number of smaller universities and colleges; at such institutions, graduate education often consists primarily of master's degree programs offered in the evening or off campus for teachers and other professionals. In major research universities, however, the functions of graduate education and continuing education not only are assigned to different offices but also are commonly viewed as occupying quite different worlds. Graduate deans are regarded as being at the center, if not the apex, of the institution—the ultimate guardians of academic quality, the protectors of tradition, and therefore somewhat inflexible and slow to change. Continuing education deans often are seen as presiding over marginal activities, which are more public services than higher education and are occasionally of questionable quality. Both of these views, in fact, are fallacious.

The term *continuing education*, as used in this chapter, is defined rather generously as embracing all teaching and learning activities conducted by colleges and universities other than the credit courses taught on campus for traditional (that is, eighteen to twenty-four-year-old, full-time) students.

M. J. Pelczar, L. C. Solmon (Eds.). *Keeping Graduate Programs Responsive to National Needs.*
New Directions for Higher Education, no. 46. San Francisco: Jossey-Bass, June 1984.

Over the years, graduate deans actually have been at the forefront in dealing with (1) adult students, (2) part-time learners, (3) students who continue their education over extended periods of time, and (4) "nontraditional" teaching-learning situations (such as tutorials, independent study, apprenticeships, and distance education). Graduate students may work with someone other than a full-time member of the university faculty on a research project in another part of the country or the world. And they often receive academic credit while laboring over dissertations many miles away from a campus, conferring with major professors by mail, telephone, computer, or an occasional trip to their offices. In the future, graduate deans may be reqired to demonstrate even greater adaptability.

Deans of continuing education in major universities often preside over operations that are quite large (with annual budgets in the $20 million to $30 million range) and that are extremely diversified, including noncredit, undergraduate and graduate credit, and advanced continuing professional education programs. Among their varied responsibilities are such activities as summer sessions, evening schools, weekend colleges, off-campus centers, training programs contracted with the military and with business and industry, correspondence courses, independent study via telecommunications, and conferences and institutes. And continuing education is increasingly moving to the center of the university's functions and purposes.

Trends Favoring Continuing Education

Adults between the ages of thirty-five and forty-four are the fastest-growing age group in the United States, increasing by 30 percent between 1980 and 1990, while the eighteen to twenty-four year-old group will be declining by 16 percent in the same period. The majority of college students are more than twenty-one years old, with 36 percent age twenty-five and over. The university population will continue to grow older in the years ahead.

Part-time students, most of them adults, already have become the dominant group in most universities. The National Center for Education Statistics reports that part-time students have increased at an average rate of 4.9 percent a year over the past seven years, while the average increases for full-time students was 2.3 percent; and that trend is expected to continue and accelerate.

Noncredit learning is the most rapidly growing educational activity in universities, and continuing professional education leads the way. Harvard University, for example, each year serves about 45,000 part-time, adult students—doctors, lawyers, business executives, educators, and other professionals learning the latest developments in their field. Graduate education increasingly will have to focus on serving practitioners in need of in-service education.

New technologies—such as computers, satellites, videotapes, and cable televison—are combining with the telephone and the duplicator to provide an integrated electronic system capable of linking professors, students, libraries, and data bases whatever they might be and of making it possible for the first time to offer truly individualized instruction. President Steven Muller (1983) of Johns Hopkins University says we have entered the age of the "Post-Gutenberg University."

Universities face new competition, even at the graduate level. The Rand Graduate Institute for Policy Studies and the Arthur D. Little Management Education Institution are accredited Ph.D.-granting institutions, and the Wang Institute is awaiting accreditation. In the military, the Army Command and General Staff College (Kansas) and the Defense Intelligence College (Washington, D.C.) offer master's degrees, and the Air Force Institute of Technology (Ohio) grants both master's and doctorate degrees.

Changes in funding also are affecting graduate education. State financial support has declined in most regions of the country, and state agencies are looking critically at graduate programs with low enrollments. The federal government has cut back its support of graduate education and research, except in defense-related and few other areas. Universities are turning to business and industry for more funding, but corporations want research and training that will serve their special needs.

Implications for Graduate Education

The cumulative effect of all these changes is likely to be a significant shift in institutional priorities over the next few years, with very real implications for graduate education. For example:

1. *Universities of necessity will devote more attention to technology transfer.* In order to obtain sufficient financial support for research, institutions will have to do more in the way of translating research findings and transmitting them to potential users. This will involve continuing education—workshops, seminars, and teleconferences. The Pennsylvania State University already has a successful technology transfer program, Pennsylvania Technical Assistance Programs (PENNTAP).

2. *Professional schools increasingly will emphasize continuing professional education.* Some professions, notably medicine and law, are producing more practitioners than is considered desirable. All professions are faced with the reality that practitioners must continue their learning throughout their professional lives. This fact is reinforced by state relicensure laws and professional recertification requirements. Many professional schools already are increasingly involved in offering continuing education for practicing professionals. These learning opportunities often are sponsored in collaboration with state or national professional societies—for example, the Practice Audit Model Project at the Pennsylvania State University, funded by the W. K. Kellogg Foundation.

3. *Universities are beginning to see adult and part-time students as important priorities.* Acknowledging this development, the American Council on Education (ACE) has established a Commission on Higher Education and the Adult Learner. ACE and the National University Continuing Education Association are sponsoring a project, with financing from the Fund for the Improvement of Postsecondary Education and the Arthur Vining Davis Foundation, to develop and disseminate a "Self-Study Assessment and Planning Guide for Postsecondary Institutions Serving Adult Learners." Other national associations are featuring sessions at their annual meetings and special conferences on such topics as the adult student, nontraditional students, noncredit programs, off-campus programs, the new technologies, and campus-business linkages (see the listings in each issue of the *Chronicle of Higher Education*).

4. *Virtually all academic components of universities are becoming involved in continuing education.* With the decline of traditional enrollments in most fields of study and the growing practice in universities to expect "every tub to stand on its own bottom" financially, most academic deans (if not their faculties) are exploring ways to identify and serve new student constituencies—at least in credit programming. Even universities with large, centralized schools or colleges of continuing education have a substantial amount of educational outreach occurring elsewhere in the institution.

These developments have important implications for graduate deans. In many instances, they will find themselves dealing more frequently with greater numbers of older students and part-time students, third-party payers (such as employers), especially designed programs, new delivery systems, and noncredit as well as credit offerings. For the immediate future, graduate deans should see the dean of continuing education as a helpful ally. Over the long term, it appears that graduate deans should, in fact, begin to see themselves as continuing educators.

Reference

Muller, S. "The Post-Gutenberg University." Paper presented to the American Association for Higher Education, Spring 1983.

Kenneth E. Young is executive director of the
National University Continuing Education Association.

Tests of knowledge and skills will reflect new content and new technologies in response to dramatic changes in learning environments.

Traditional Tests for Nontraditional Students

Bernard V. Khoury

Testing is simply an effort to measure in a systematic way what, if anything, a person has learned from an educational experience. Although testing often involves a structured opportunity to answer questions orally or in written form, its most important manifestation is a practical display of some ability to perform a task, such as repairing a plumbing leak, or solving an engineering problem, or assisting an accident victim, or preparing a meal.

In the traditional academic environment of schools and universities, testing has usually referred to paper-and-pencil responses to questions designed to measure learning that has occurred in the classroom. In this environment, the primary purpose of most tests is to determine if the student displays sufficient mastery of some material to allow him or her to proceed to the next step in the educational ladder, which in turn, will be evaluated by another test to determine access to the next learning experience, and so on.

New Uses for Tests

While tests have traditionally been reviewed as devices to determine admissibility to the next academic course or the next educational

M. J. Pelczar, L. C. Solmon (Eds.). *Keeping Graduate Programs Responsive to National Needs.*
New Directions for Higher Education, no. 46. San Francisco: Jossey-Bass, June 1984.

level, they are increasingly being used for purposes of guidance, placement, measurement of competency, and certification.

In addition to serving this growing variety of purposes, tests
must increasingly reflect the diversity of means by which students have
acquired skills and knowledge. While classroom learning may warrant
testing a student on the historical evolution of procedure or a skill, for
example, a plumber's effectiveness is probably not significantly influenced by his or her knowledge of water closets during the 1930s, but
a cook may need to know about kitchen utensils in colonial America in
order to work at a restaurant in Williamsburg. Likewise, knowledge of
bridge construction in the Roman Empire might be of questionable
value to a professional engineer in 1984. Students can now use a growing range of communications and technologies in order to learn, so
tests must begin to focus on the explicit learning objectives rather than
on the process that has led to the achievement of those objectives. The
answer to a particular question may be much more important than the
process used in deriving the answer — a feature that will be unsettling to
some teachers.

New Environment for Tests

Testing is not an end in itself but a means to facilitate, improve,
or assess an educational process. It can only be justified if it contributes
somehow to better plumbing, more effective engineering, improved
health care, or better meals. Thus, the development of new tests must
recognize the deinstitutionalization of education. Students of all ages
are learning less and less from classroom and teaching environments
and more and more from less structured learning environments. We
can expect to see dramatic changes in learning stimulated by new technologies, personal computers, cable television, videodiscs, and electronic universities. Teaching will continue to be important for many
age groups and many areas of study, but what and how teachers teach
will be less important than what and how learners learn. Again, testing
will need to focus on the outcomes of learning and not on the process by
which the learning takes place.

Commentors may usefully discuss the somewhat philosophic
question of whether education should leave the classroom. The key
issue here, however, is the fact that education — or more properly, learning — is leaving the classroom and our traditional teaching institutions; it occurs increasingly in learning institutions such as the home,
the office, the electronics library, the learning center, the factory, and
the kitchen.

In an environment in which education and learning are deinstitutionalized and the product becomes more important than process, and in which teaching is recognized as only one means toward learning, then the testing of such learning must reflect at least three features: more precise specification of learning objectives, less focus on the ability to learn, and use of new technologies.

Testing in the New Environment

In light of increasingly diverse modes of learning, tests must be based even more clearly on precisely defined learning or behavioral outcomes. Furthermore, these outcomes or objectives must be widely, if not universally, understood so that credentials are transferable from one institution or geographic setting to another. While some learners may seek testing as a way of personally validating their knowledge, most learners will have a more practical purpose of obtaining a credential or formal record of their accomplishments.

Because the processes of education are much easier to measure and to validate, the products of education have not drawn adequate attention from traditional teaching institutions. Consistent with this marginal focus on the products of education, the most widely used tests in higher education have measured student aptitude or ability to learn. Such aptitude measures are often used to admit students to a teaching or a process-oriented institution. They clearly become less relevant in an environment that focuses on what has been learned rather than on the process by which the learning occurs. Hence, renewed efforts will need to be directed to the measurement of current knowledge and abilities and not the potential or ability to learn.

As learning occurs increasingly away from educational institutions, then so too should tests of that learning. Paper and pencil tests will give way to tests using more comtemporary media, such as computer-based video and audio devices. Interactive electronics will allow innovative tests of skills and abilities that are not amenable to standard paper and pencil tests (especially those that are multiple choice). Such new technologies will provide virtually instantaneous modification and adaptation of test content as well as immediate reports on performance.

Tests are merely one part of a complex and changing educational and learning system. As the substance and the techniques of learning change, so too will the contents and the delivery of tests. Through all of these changes, increasing attention can and will be given to the questions of who has learned and what and how well learned was the lesson.

Bernard V. Khoury served as the Graduate Record Examination executive program director at the Educational Testing Service. He is now associate vice-president for academic affairs at the University of Maryland.

*Universities are challenged to maintain the essential
fabric of graduate education while taking advantage of the
opportunities occasioned by university-industry arrangements.*

University and Industry
as Partners

James C. Seferis
Luther S. Williams

An Industrial Affiliate Program

A specific example of an industrial affiliate program funded by
the National Science Foundation (NSF) is a project that has focused on
the structure property relations of the crystalline polymer polypropylene. The collaboration was initiated between the Department of
Chemical Engineering at the University of Washington and one of
Hercules's top research scientists in structure property relations. (Hercules is known as the world leader in the production of polypropylene.)
The research scientist provided support both in terms of materials and
in the problem definition. He was also instrumental in acquiring
management commitment to the project as well as in carefully defining
the extent of participation of his institution. Commitment was made in
terms of well-characterized samples, equipment, personnel time, and

M. J. Pelczar, L. C. Solmon (Eds.). *Keeping Graduate Programs Responsive to National Needs.*
New Directions for Higher Education, no. 46. San Francisco: Jossey-Bass, June 1984.

supplies when they were needed. To further facilitate the interaction, the Department of Chemical Engineering gave the research scientist an affiliate professorship at the University of Washington; this appointment provided the needed recognition of the cooperation from both the industrial and the academic points of view.

The NSF program that funded this collaboration provides an incentive for conducting research with industry in an academic environment because it includes the peer review process that is well accepted within academic circles. Also, by having the project sponsored through NSF, we avoided the traditional cliché that industrially sponsored research is more "applied" than it is "fundamental." For young faculty members who will be judged on their research for promotion and eventual tenure, this is significant. Such a project, then, can strongly establish their academic credentials while allowing them to interact with industry in a way that helps their research to grow. On the other hand, the whole concept of one-on-one research projects in collaboration with industry relies on successful interactions that must be initiated and maintained throughout the life of the project. To ensure that this is indeed provided within the university structure, the Department of Chemical Engineering at the University of Washington has institutionalized such relationships with industry, providing continuous opportunities for faculty and students to interact with their counterparts from the chemical industry. Thus, this industrial affiliate program is not designed for the sole purpose of raising funds. Although it is successful in that respect also, it has no set fee, and its primary purpose is indeed to facilitate interaction with industry. Its success is evident from the fact that over thirty national and international chemical companies are now members of the program. Numerous research projects with industry, cosponsored by the NSF's Industry/University Cooperative (IUC) program, have been initiated by the faculty of the department through the affiliate program, which also attests to its success.

Equal access to the resources of the program by the faculty is ensured by utilizing the industrial affiliate program funds exclusively to support incoming graduate students to the department before they choose a specific funded research project offered by an individual faculty member. This method of distribution also provides flexibility in responding to fluctuations in income that should be expected with these types of programs.

James C. Seferis is director of the Industrial Affiliate Program in Chemical Engineering and founder of the Polymer Composite Laboratory of the University of Washington.

Problems and Benefits for Graduate Training
of University-Industry Relationships

Industrial support of graduate study and university research programs is an activity of long standing, but the contemporary setting of these partnerships derives from the substantially increased level of interactions between industry and university-based graduate training and research. Significant among the explanations for an expansion of university-industry programs is the less-than-positive state of the graduate education enterprise. The past decade has represented an era of considerable challenges to graduate education. Prominent among these are a decreased and more heterogeneous applicant pool, a substantial reduction in federally sponsored graduate training programs, and increasingly obsolete scientific equipment and inadequate research facilities as against the increased aggregate cost of graduate study. Moreover, the heightened interface of research and graduate training with national priorities and needs as reflected in national productivity and international economic competition has occasioned greater attention to the qualitative as well as quantitative dimensions of graduate study. Thus, in an effort to address the existing difficulties and respond to the challenges of the eighties, a new set of mechanisms has emerged that is characterized by a more stringent intermeshing of graduate education and university-based research with the categorical needs and interests of specific industries.

To maintain the integrity of the academic institution and the graduate education process in particular, considerable attention and deliberations have been given to the nature of university-industry agreements. Critical to such deliberation are issues related to the freedom of inquiry and the timely communication (that is, publication) of scientific findings, as contrasted with the protection of the industry's need to ascertain the potential patentability of technical developments. Such deliberations have focused on the public disclosure of results vis-à-vis the patent process, financial responsibility for potential patenting processes, definitions of property ownership and royalties distribution, exclusive license of patents resulting from the industry-sponsored research and graduate training partnership, collaborative (shared) research time and resources, and information transfer between the participating institutions.

The obvious benefits of such partnerships include the provision of increased resources for research and graduate training, the substantial commitment of university expertise to an array of major research problems, and a more highly interfaced university-industry form of technology transfer. Clearly, all of the above should promote enhanced use of national resources, which at a first approximation, is sufficiently important to motivate the potential partners to address the problem areas associated with such ventures.

On the other hand, contemporary graduate training and research programs (such as biotechnology) must be incorporated within the steady-state graduate operation without curricula and resource adjustments that decrease the quality of other essential graduate training programs. Furthermore, these new programs must maintain the balance of the aggregate responsibility of university faculty members for teaching and institutional services as well as for research. Thus, the participation of faculty members in industry-sponsored research should be characterized by assessments of the potential reduction of their efforts in the instructional area. Perhaps of even greater significance are the programmatic and organizational arrangements (departmental, interdepartmental, program, and school level) necessary for the conduct of specific research efforts mandated by the partnerships. The potential difficulty lies in the imposition of a highly specific industry-sponsored research program on a university structure characterized by a more expansive and less specialized approach to graduate training and research.

In many instances, industry-sponsored research obligates scholarly linkages between otherwise quite independent scholars. In such instances, the possible difficulty experienced by graduate students whose training typically occurs in a single mentor-graduate student relationship is considerable. Moreover, while the issue of free inquiry and open exchange of information and generic research materials is vital to the professional interests of the faculty member, a restrictive operating agreement offers profound consequences for the scholar in training (that is, for graduate students and postdoctoral fellows). In particular, it is critically important that graduate students and postdoctoral fellows be allowed to engage in essentially unlimited explorations of basic questions evidenced by the studies without risks of negative assessments as regards their scholarly productivity. In addition, the opportunity to submit findings to peer-reviewed publication processes must be preserved, the proprietary nature of the industry-sponsored research notwithstanding.

Thus, while substantial attention has been devoted to the desirability of explicit guidelines for the establishment of university-industry arrangements, there remains a significant organizational matter, unrelated to proprietary information, patents, royalties, consultantships, and exchanges of information that must be addressed: The traditional precepts and objectives of graduate training may make the highly selective and focused industry-sponsored research contracts undesirable. The most reasonable accommodation of the interests of both partners, then, lies in broadly based industrial support of basic or fundamental research. Under such a support, specific resources are designated for graduate student training, faculty scholarship, equipment, and so on as components of an overall program.

Universities can readily accommodate industry-sponsored announced partnerships are consistent with this programmatic focus; specific (targeted) contracts awarded to several investigators. Moreover, a partnership characterized by such a broadly based research program need not constrain industry from commercializing products that result from these research programs. Interestingly, several recently announced partnerships are consistent with this programmatic focus; they include the McDonnell Douglas Foundation support of the neurobiology program of Washington University's School of Medicine, the IBM-sponsored faculty fellowship in computer sciences awarded to various universities, and the Beckman-sponsored postdoctoral training program in molecular biology at the University of California at Irvine. Hopefully, these examples are representative of future partnerships that will be structured to effect the optimal interinstitutional arrangements between otherwise distinct institutions.

Luther S. Williams is vice-president for academic affairs and dean of the University System Graduate School at the University of Colorado.

*Although much federal support for higher education exists,
its relationship to developing innovative programs is
quantitatively and qualitatively different among various
fields and disciplines.*

The Federal Role in
Graduate Program Innovation

Thomas J. Linney, Jr.

In the recent history of graduate education, there have been many
direct federal influences on program innovation. Most of the funding
for such program innovation has now expired. Some legislative
authority remains, but most programs are unfunded and expected to
remain that way for some time. Still, even without direct authority, the
federal government plays a considerable role in graduate program
innovation. This chapter discusses the role and influence of the federal
government on innovation in graduate programs.

   After four years of domestic spending cuts and legislative limi-
tation on spending authority for most programs related to higher
education, it is admittedly a difficult task to argue that there is an
essential federal role in graduate program innovation. Certainly it is
not an overt role. The visible programs that show federal support for
innovation, such as National Science Foundation grants for departmental improvement, the Fund for the Improvement of Postsecondary
Education, and grants for program or course development flowing
from the National Endowments for the Arts and Humanities, have all
been reduced or have shifted their priorities away from program development in graduate education. Yet, even as this low point has been

M. J. Pelczar, L. C. Solmon (Eds.). *Keeping Graduate Programs Responsive to National Needs.*
New Directions for Higher Education, no. 46. San Francisco: Jossey-Bass, June 1984.

reached, other federal agencies have been increasing support for research and development activities. For example, new signs of a quickening of interest in the elastic character of graduate education have been visible in programs housed in the Department of Defense and the National Institutes of Health and in selected parts of the National Science Foundation.

This ebb and flow repeats a common pattern in federal support — a pattern not often appreciated on the campus, where consistent, predictable support is regarded as the most desirable. The fact is that, despite some appearances of imperviousness, federal spending priorities are flexible, and the last six years have seen relatively rapid shifts in federal priorities. These have been accompanied by a range of shifts in support for research spending. And research spending provides the most direct line of relationship between any federal role and graduate program innovation.

In the four decades following World War II, this country has evolved from a nation where less than 10 percent of the population benefited from higher education to a time where 50 percent of high school graduates now enroll in some form of postsecondary education. This has caused tremendous expansion in the network of graduate program offerings and has served as a stimulus for many kinds of new programs and innovations adopted to serve the changing character of graduate education. Adjustments and displacements caused by this growth are still being felt throughout the graduate community.

Role Conflict

As the midpoint of the eighties approaches, conflict in the federal role in innovation has become apparent; such conflict follows from the two directions in federal policy about advanced education that have been visible over the past four decades.

One direction is the continuation of federal support for research and development through the so-called mission agencies of the federal government. Six federal departments or agencies provide the majority of support for research funding at the graduate level in the nation's colleges and universities. The Departments of Agriculture, Energy, Defense, and Health and Human Services (principally through the National Institutes of Health), with the National Science Foundation and the National Aeronautics and Space Administration, support the research programs, research facilities, fellowships, and traineeships that provide several billion dollars in annual support toward the development of new knowledge and the production of a succeeding generation of scholars.

Replication is a certain outcome of these investments. The lineage between graduate education and research is what makes possible the replication and expansion of the fields and disciplines supported by these agencies. Note, however, that not all fields and disciplines are equally supported by federal research efforts.

For a combination of reasons, including budget priorities, economic recessions, and shifting labor needs, some areas of scholarship and academic learning are supported at much lower levels than others. Currently, support for the arts, humanities, and social sciences is at a low point, all the more visible because of the changes in relative standing among fields and disciplines. To add to the current confusion, academic interest remains high in some of the currently underfunded areas like the social sciences, where a body of knowledge and a body of scholars continue to multiply in spite of lagging levels of federal support.

Meanwhile, federal support of students has continued to grow; this is the second direction that federal policy takes. Starting in the fifties with National Defense Education Act fellowships and loans, expanding into more loans and work study programs in the sixties, and expanding to grants and more loans and work study in the seventies, the federal government now invests over $5 billion a year in support of students in postsecondary education. Only a fraction of that amount supports graduate education, where guaranteed student loans provide the majority of federal support. Even smaller amounts provide for innovation at any level. Still, it is hard to imagine operating any kind of college or university in the absence of federal student aid. This, too, is a development of the last four decades.

Federal Roles in Innovation

The two policy directions of federal support provide two major mechanisms for support of innovation and change in graduate education. Clearly, research support results in changing priorities among the fields and disciplines in which major support is available. Thus, the shifting patterns of support influence new areas of study, which, in turn, open up new fields of research and ultimately cause entire areas of disciplined scholarship to be modified or to multiply in response to new discoveries. Some of these new areas have developed as a direct result of federal support; some have developed as a result of increased state-of-the art knowledge and equipment that have been transferred from other discipline areas. For example, the physical sciences enjoyed broad support in the fifties and sixties as military and civilian space programs engaged the focus of resources; the biological sciences and health-related fields currently enjoy a similar era of broad support. This shift in support has resulted in such a combination of the two disciplines as biochemistry, where knowledge of a physical science is expanded through its application to biological fields.

Innovation, then, is supported both through new areas of research support and through new combinations of knowledge that broaden the mold of graduate education and research. The indirect role of the federal government should be acknowledged, but local decisions over the use and combining of resources also play a large role in the directions taken by new programs. Competitive research strategies, for example, provide mutual stimulation of programs and universities.

In other areas not driven by federal investments in research, the role of the federal government in innovation is less clear. Some support for the arts and humanities is derived through the programs of the National Endowments for the Arts and Humanities, but their support levels are small and the universe of their support mission extends well beyond colleges and universities to other instruments of culture that may lack a direct connection to graduate education. The Fund for the Improvement of Postsecondary Education (FIPSE) in the Department of Education provides a small amount of impetus for innovation in higher education. However, FIPSE's mission is broad, and graduate program innovation has received little attention from this group. Recent FIPSE guideline changes have increased the priority of graduate program innovation, but it will take some years for a new pattern of support to develop.

The Market as Innovator

The absence of federal support for large areas of the arts, humanities, and social sciences has led to a different kind of stimulus for innovation. In these areas, support for innovation has come from the marketplace of student enrollment as colleges and universities scramble to find new ways to increase students in fields and disciplines with uncertain connections to national priorities. Many of these innovations are discussed elsewhere in this volume. Federal student assistance provides some support for graduate students in the form of eligibility for need-based loans and work study programs, but this support is currently limited to students attending graduate programs at least half time, and not all campuses allow graduate students to participate in these programs. Federally guaranteed loans may make up the biggest federal contribution of support in these areas. Some 40 percent of all graduate students borrow under federal loan programs, and an estimated 25 percent of the loan volume of these programs flows to graduate and professional students. This accounts for something in excess of $2 billion a year in loan funds. Thus, to the extent that the individual student is willing to go into debt, support does exist for advanced levels of education. And this support indirectly contributes to graduate programs and innovation when combined with institutional support reflecting a policy of moving into new areas of graduate study.

Thomas J. Linney, Jr., is associated with the Council of Graduate Schools in the United States.

The way in which graduate education is conducted affects the development of socially responsible men and women as well as their competence.

Graduate Education and Social Responsibility

Howard R. Bowen

Historically, graduate schools have been confined to the traditional arts and sciences and engaged primarily in training college teachers. But, in recent decades, they have branched out into numerous applied fields— for example, agriculture, business, communications, computer science, criminal justice, education, engineering, fine arts, forestry, health professions, home economics, library science, and public affairs. Moreover, most fields that were part of the traditional arts and sciences have taken on practical applications other than college teaching. Especially is this so of the natural sciences, economics, and psychology. The various departments of the graduate school thus have become small professional schools comparable in most respects to the traditional schools of medicine, law, and theology. They are each training grounds for people who aspire to professional careers. This chapter, then, approaches the subject of social responsibility from the point of view of professional education, whether it takes place in departments of graduate school of arts and sciences or whether it occurs in separate professional schools. In other words, what I have to say is as applicable to a school of law or medicine as it is to a department of history, chemistry, or computer science.

M. J. Pelczar, L. C. Solmon (Eds.). *Keeping Graduate Programs Responsive to National Needs.*
New Directions for Higher Education, no. 46. San Francisco: Jossey-Bass, June 1984.

The social responsibilities of a professional department or school are long established and quite simple. They are also noncontroversial — at least in theory, though not always in practice. There are two basic responsibilities, one technical and the other moral.

The first of these is the obligation of a professional department or school to turn out technically competent practitioners. An incompetent professional is an abomination. Competent people are well trained, they have capacity for growth, they are thorough and self-disciplined, they are aware of their limitations, and they feel an obligation to go on learning. Sustained competence, however, also requires that they have a strong sense of vocation, which means literally that they be "called" to their profession.

The second of these responsibilities is the obligation to turn out men and women of broad learning and culture who will join the leadership of the society and will exert a constructive influence in community and civic life. These people exhibit humane sensibilities in their contacts with other individuals, they accept responsibility relating to the affairs of the community and the nation, and they can be entrusted with the lives and fortunes of others.

These two responsibilities are, of course, ideals that professional programs are obliged to strive for, but, like all worthwhile ideals, they are not fully attainable in the real world.

What are the means available to professional schools and departments to attain these ideals? The principal ones are the recruitment and selection of students, the recruitment and selection of faculty, the curriculum, and the campus environment. Each of these means raises further issues pertaining to the social responsibility of graduate departments or schools.

Recruitment and Selection of Students

Every professional school or department faces conflict values connected with student recruitment and selection. On the one hand, there are pressures or incentives to increase enrollments. Some of these come from within, as schools or departments seek to augment tuition income or state appropriations or simply seek the aggrandizement that comes with size. Some pressures come from the internal sense of obligation to open up opportunity for young persons — especially women and minorities — or from the external force of affirmative action. Tendencies toward large size may derive also from the belief that a school or department should be guided by market demand and not attempt to impose quotas based on manpower estimates (usually of dubious validity).

On the other hand, there are pressures to hold down or reduce enrollments. Outside practitioners or their associations may hope to control enrollment as a way of protecting monopoly positions or of restraining competition. Funding agencies sometimes place limitations on enrollments as a way of reducing expenditures. Internally, there may be a view that admissions criteria should be rigorous enough to encourage undergraduate colleges to provide well-educated candidates. The problem of every school or department is to thread its way through these conflicting interests and to end up with a socially responsible solution.

Some help in reaching the right decision can be found by referring back to the basic objectives: to produce competent practitioners and to turn out socially responsible men and women. If professional educators will seriously accept these twin goals, the "right" decisions on the recruitment and selection of students will follow. These goals imply, for example, that admission should be limited to people who have the potential to become competent, admission practices should not exclude qualified minorities and women, that a graduate school should not be party to restraint of competition or to growth for its own sake, and that admissions criteria should be encouraging to sound high school and college preparation. There are, of course, differences of opinion on the meanings of "competent" and "socially responsible," but it is the duty of professional educators to make these interpretations.

Recruitment and Selection of Faculty

The second means available to professional programs for attaining the two ideals is the selection of faculty. The influence of teachers derives not only from what they teach but from who they are. The objectives of most faculty members lean strongly toward technical competence and scholarly achievement in a relatively narrow subspeciality. They see their task as conveying the substance and outlook of that field to their students, to their professional peers, and sometimes to the general public.

On the other hand, some faculty members rise above technique. Some convey the relationship of their specialities to the broader range of knowledge, some bring out moral questions that flow from their subject, some convey love of learning and passion for the truth, some take an interest in the all-round personal development of their students.

I do not mean that students invariably adopt the values exhibited by faculty. They may sometimes be repelled by them. I also do not mean that students are influenced by every faculty member they encounter. Sometimes only a few or even a single teacher may become a model or mentor who exerts decisive influence on students. As Miller and Orr (1980) have written, "It is not only in systematic ethical argument, political addresses, and sermons that moral images are enunciated. Moral images are also manifested in the lives of individuals who populate communities, whether religious or academic" (p. 14).

The academic community, especially in the research universities, tends to be suspicious of efforts to select faculty on the basis of their personal character or their interest in students. As Derek Bok has observed (1982) "Even with the awakening interest in ethics, no research university could hope to reinstate character as a basis for appointments. The criterion is simply too susceptible to abuse, too vague, too remote from the primary commitment to learning and discovery" (p. 122). This warning should not be ignored. I think, however, that Bok overstates the case. For one thing, many institutions, while following their usual selection procedures, manage — by accident perhaps — to appoint some broadly educated, humane, and cultivated people who are at the same time technically brilliant. There are many professors who care about ethical issues related to their professional fields and who are concerned for students. Professional excellence and humane sensibilities are not necessarily incompatible. There are thousands of examples of such people already in academic life, and it would be no offense for institutions to tilt their selection procedures a bit toward persons who exhibit ethical and social concerns. Even without doing that, it would be wise for them to encourage and reward such people who happen to have joined the faculty.

Curriculum

The third means of attaining the two ideals is the curriculum, including course offerings, degree requirements, and methods of instruction. Most of the literature on the teaching of professional ethics warns against direct exhortation and indoctrination. It is widely agreed that moral issues should be woven into the regular technical courses as they arise naturally. They should be treated in the spirit of free and open discussion of all points of view and not in a doctrinaire fashion, though there is no inhibition against professors revealing their own views.

Every course, no matter how factual or technical, may be taught in a way that touches on values. At the very minimum, any course may influence, either positively or negatively, such values as respect for truth, thoroughness, and self-discipline. And, in most courses, a broader range of value questions are readily present and can be naturally brought to the surface. At the same time, any course, no matter how laden with values, can be taught in a way that emphasizes factual knowledge and technique and plays down value questions. Sadly, even the most humanistic subjects, such as literature, philosophy, religion, or history, can be, and often are, taught in ways that ignore or play down questions of value.

In recent years, there has been something of a movement among professional schools of law, medicine, business, and other fields toward offering courses on professional ethics and toward including at least one such course in the degree requirements. Donald Callahan and Sissela Bok (1980) have edited a useful book of readings describing and evaluating this movement. Among those involved in teaching applied ethics, there is general agreement that these courses should involve wide-ranging analysis and discussion of ethical issues and avoid the pitfalls of indoctrination. It is also generally agreed that there is a shortage of faculty who are adequately prepared to give these courses. Derek Bok's (1982) conclusions on the matter strike me as both discerning and graceful:

> What can we say about the effect of such courses on the lives of students and the moral quality of the society? In candor, we cannot answer with certainty. But certainty has never been the criterion for educational decisions. Every professor knows that much of the material conveyed in the classroom will soon be forgotten. The willingness to continue teaching must always rest upon an act of faith that students will retain a useful conceptual framework, a helpful approach to the subject, a valuable method of analysis, or some other intangible residue of lasting intellectual value. Much the same is true of courses on ethical problems. It does not seem plausible to suppose that such classes will help students become more alert in perceiving ethical issues, more aware of the reasons underlying moral principles, and more equipped to reason carefully in applying these principles to concrete cases. Will they behave more ethically? One would suppose so, provided we assume that most students have a desire to lead ethical lives and share the basic moral values common to our society. Granted, we cannot *prove* that such results will be achieved. Even so, the prospects are surely great enough to warrant a determined effort, not only because the subject matter is interesting and the problems intellectually challenging but also because the goal is so important to the quality of the society in which we live [pp. 134–135].

Institutional Environment

Finally, in considering the means of attaining the twin ideals of professional competence and social responsibility, one should not overlook the institutional environment. This includes the physical features of the campus, the prevailing patterns of extracurricular life, the common attitudes, the characteristics of the student peer group, the traditions handed down from the past, and, by no means least, the decisions and actions of the faculty and administration and the basic values underlying them.

Institutional environments convey values more or less spontaneously. They send signals to students — sometimes very subtle signals — about the values that are accepted, tolerated, or discouraged. Environments also provide many experiences — in the concert hall, museum, chapel, residence hall, or on the playing field — that help to form values.

The environment has the advantage that most parts of it are optional. It does not overtly preach or teach and is flexible enough to allow a range of behavior. But it is always there, exerting a quiet but persistent and, in the long run, effective influence on the way people think and believe and behave, not only in their student days but throughout their lives.

It is a pity that college environments have in recent decades become less effective in the sense that millions of students, the part-time commuters, cannot partake of campus influences and facilities as fully as they are available to full-time residential students. The traditional power of the college or graduate school to transmit values grew in large measure out of residential campus life with its opportunity for contact with professors, informal conversation, cultural experiences, and use of libraries, laboratories, and museums.

To carry out its responsibility in the formation of values, higher education must find ways of bringing more students to the campus as full-time residents or, when this is not possible, of finding substitutes for full-time campus residence. The traditional residential college or university was an elite institution and bears some of the opprobrium attached to elitism. The ideal to be sought is to bring to large numbers of people the ambience of the residential campus or the best possible substitute.

Concluding Cautionary Comments

Despite the need for greater attention to values and the signs of increasing interest, four cautionary comments are in order (Bowen,

1982). First, the academic community is not of a single mind either on the possibility of affecting values through higher education or on the desirability of including the transmittal of values among the objectives of our colleges and universities. Many academic people are engrossed in their technical specialties and scholarly endeavors and do not acknowledge responsibility for the values acquired by their students.

Second, it is generally agreed that there are severe limitations on the amount of influence colleges and universities can expect to exert on the values of students — even with the best of intentions and the best of techniques. The college experience is only one of many influences on values, and it occurs at a time in students' lives when their values have already been largely and, to some extent, irrevocably formed.

Third, even when practicing educators wish to do something about values, knowledge of how to proceed is precarious.

Fourth, most of the obvious techniques for education in values are of doubtful efficacy. One of these methods is exhortation, a form of which is crude indoctrination; another is the objective study or analysis of values. Neither of these techniques appears to result in the internalization of values. Merely knowing the good deed is not readily transformed into doing the good deed. Apparently, subtler techniques are more useful — for example, encouraging the free discussion of issues, dilemmas, and alternatives, or putting students into contact with approriate mentors, or providing an environment that is supportive of sound ethical and esthetic values.

Any college or university that attempts to influence the values of its students will do well to heed these disclaimers. Nevertheless, the task is eminently worth attempting, and it is of vital importance to our society that it be attempted.

References

Bok, D. *Beyond the Ivory Tower.* Cambridge, Mass.: Harvard University Press, 1982.
Bowen, H. R. *The State of the Nation and the Agenda for Higher Education.* San Francisco: Jossey-Bass, 1982.
Callahan, D., and Bok, S. (Eds.) *Ethics Teaching in Higher Education.* New York: Plenum, 1980.
Miller, D. E., and Orr, J. B. "Beyond the Relativism Myth." *Change,* October 1980, p. 14.

Howard R. Bowen is the R. Stanton Avery Professor of Economics and Education at the Claremont Graduate School.

Index